Mary Page Greene enjoyed getting to know several relatives, visiting ancestral homes, and learning much United States history while writing this story. She plays tennis and tends her garden in southwest Virginia while researching her next book. She has two children and two grandchildren.

To my grandparents, Ann and Jim Greene, for their sacrifices to benefit future generations.

Mary Page Greene

DADDY BEAR GOES TO WAR

WWII Chronicle with his Cartoons

AUSTIN MACAULEY PUBLISHERS™

LONDON * CAMBRIDGE * NEW YORK * SHARJAH

Ordering Information
Quantity sales: Special discounts are available on quantity purchases by corporations, associations, and others. For details, contact the publisher at the address below.

Publisher's Cataloging-in-Publication data
Greene, Mary Page
Daddy Bear Goes to War

ISBN 9781685626808 (Paperback)
ISBN 9781685626815 (ePub e-book)

Library of Congress Control Number: 2023904491

www.austinmacauley.com/us

First Published 2023
Austin Macauley Publishers LLC
40 Wall Street 33rd Floor, Suite 3302
New York, NY 10005
USA

mail-usa@austinmacauley.com
+1 (646) 5125767

It took years of starts and stops to reach this point while several people supported my endeavor. I am grateful to all of them for their help. Early on my aunt, Ann Greene Hodges, gave me the scrapbook her mother compiled and the letters she saved. My father, William Greene, signed the request for his father's official military records. Fortunately, they still existed. The VMI Museum gave me my grandfather's student file. My cousins, Florence (Penny) Marshall Mallory, Mary Mallory Marshall Sisson, Martha Custis Peter, and John Walker gave me cartoons, photographs, and family documents. Penny took me on a tour of family residences in Washington, D.C. and told me about our relatives and ancestors. Larry Williams gave me a tour and history of Spring Hill Farm in Hamilton, VA where my grandfather was born.

Mary Atwell gave me critical guidance in organizing the material and shepherded me along as the story developed. Penny and King Mallory, Michelle and Lawrence McConnell, Ann Martyn, Frank O'Brien, Angie Kayte, Katie McKernan, and Tom Walker gave me valuable input.

My brother and his wife, Sylvia and William Greene, my sister and brother-in-law, Joy and Dave Gwaltney, and several friends, Laurie Walker Pike, Agnes Skellington, Suzy Farhat, Linda Nelson, Teik Phillips, and Mary Copp listened and encouraged me for many years. Finally, my late husband, Joe Gwaltney, was very supportive of this project and the research that was necessary.

Table of Contents

Prologue:
The Question

The discussion leader began the conversation with the statement, "I could never leave my family and go to war."

I responded, "My grandfather did."

It's funny how a comment can inspire one to seek information about someone or something. That is how writing this story began. In the fall of 2010 at a church in Roanoke, Virginia, I attended a discussion about the book, *Unbroken*. The book is about Louis Zampereni, a runner who was training for the Olympics when he was drafted into World War II and became an aviator. He survived being lost at sea in the Pacific Ocean and three years of horrific abuse as a POW in a Japanese prison camp. After the war, he returned to the United States and struggled with alcoholism. As a result, he started a foundation and helped many young people. Years later, he returned to Japan in an act of forgiveness for his torture.

I didn't know much about World War II, just that my grandfather, known as Francis, Hanny, Jimmy, and Jim, participated. As I drove home that evening, I wanted to learn about his involvement. At a family reunion in 1996, my aunt shared some letters with cartoons that my grandfather created while serving in the war. I was intrigued with the cartoons.

Granddaddy Greene died in 1969 in Chevy Chase, Maryland, when I was 11. We lived hundreds of miles apart, so I didn't see him often. During our visits to his home, I saw his military paraphernalia from several wars, displayed in a small basement room, but I was too young to appreciate this history.

After the book discussion, I gave my aunt a call. "Hi Ann. I have a request. May I borrow Granddaddy Greene's letters? I want to learn more about him and his participation in the war."

She responded, "I would love to share the letters. You probably remember him more than his other grandchildren. Please come for a visit."

After our conversation, I drove to Ann's home in North Carolina to get the letters and began a relationship with my father's sister. As a child, I lived in six states and family dynamics prevented us from having much contact with my father's family. She shared many things about her childhood and our extended family which piqued my interest even more.

My Aunt Ann described her father as a kind, loving, generous man who was a friend to all. She showed me some of his homemade cards for many different occasions. They were evidence of his sense of humor and playfulness. She told me how much he loved his alma mater, Virginia Military Institute. His competitive spirit was evident in the hours he spent playing or watching sports. He was most at home outdoors, whether tending the rose garden or helping his children improve their skills riding a bicycle or hitting a baseball.

At age 42, shortly after the attack on Pearl Harbor, my grandfather signed up for the Air Corps, part of the U.S. Army, in his hometown of Washington, D.C. He left his wife, three small children, a prospering advertising business, and an offer to head the art department at Time magazine. Jim served his country for three years, mostly in Texas, North Africa, and Italy.

Ann gave me a couple of shoeboxes packed with about 300 letters and a scrapbook my grandmother had made. I organized, read, scanned, and transposed the letters. I found a book about his Air Corps division, the Liberandos, and learned that this group still had regular reunions. My father, my grandfather's second child, and I attended a gathering in 2013 at Wright Patterson Air Force Base in Ohio.

I subsequently requested my grandfather's official military records from the National Personnel Records Center in St. Louis, Missouri. I knew there was a slim chance that they still existed. Records were lost throughout the war when ships were sunk crossing the Atlantic Ocean. After the war, a terrible fire at the repository in St. Louis in 1973 destroyed 17 million Army and Air Force files.

In 2012, I was standing on my front porch on a sunny afternoon, listening to the sounds of summer when our longtime mailman walked up the sidewalk of our tree-lined street. He handed me a big envelope from the National Personnel Records Center. I gave him a big hug!

My grandfather's records confirmed his involvement in the war effort. To get a better understanding of his war experiences, I interviewed Colonel William McIntosh, former head of the D-Day Memorial in Bedford, Virginia, who explained the information in the documents. I read many books, particularly about the battles in the North African and European theaters.

After reading these records, I visited places that informed his life and my story. I went to the Virginia Military Institute in Lexington, Virginia to learn about his years there. He matriculated in 1917 and graduated in 1922, taking time off in 1918 to train for World War I in Plattsburgh, NY. In his college file, the high school principal stated:

Intellectual promise: Mediocre

Seriousness of purpose: Makes serious effort

Personal character: Above reproach

I contacted several relatives who knew him. Generations of his mother's family have lived in the Washington, D.C. area for over 250 years and saved many family records. They shared remembrances and correspondence. My cousin, Penny, took me on a tour of old family dwellings and Oak Hill Cemetery in the Georgetown neighborhood of Washington, D.C. I found other historical documents at the Georgetown Neighborhood Library. I was particularly interested in ancestral documents and other sources that shed light on life in Georgetown during the first half of the 20th century. The historical records traced the family's arrival in the area and their participation in the community.

I learned about my grandfather's birth at Spring Hill Farm in Hamilton, Virginia. His father committed suicide there when he was four weeks old. I visited that home and the current owner gave me a tour and the history of the farm. I have a few letters that my grandfather wrote as a child to his mother while staying at the farm during the summer. Walking around and looking at old family pictures gave me a sense of the place.

My grandfather's oldest child, my uncle, died in 1981 but his widow, Peggy, still lives in Pennsylvania. She told me of the family's long history in the northern part of the country and England. The Greenes helped settle Providence, Rhode Island, in 1636 and fought against England in the Revolutionary War. Peggy still has my great-great-grandfather's Union Navy sword hanging on the wall.

In 2015, I joined my sister in cleaning out our father's home in Danville, Virginia. I collected a box of family artifacts that gave me more information. A picture of my grandparents in 1955 in front of a house in northern New York led me to the Adams, New York community. A subsequent visit to the local historical society explained the family migration from Rhode Island to Washington, D.C. The local historians gave me obituaries for my great, great grandfather and great, great, great grandfather as well as directions to the cemetery and their graves.

The title of the book, *Daddy Bear Goes to War,* describes my grandfather. His love for his family is seen throughout his many letters, and his illustrations reveal his positive attitude, sense of humor and playfulness. His war record and other information shed light on the character and personality of a man who served his country when duty called and compassionately led thousands of men. For example, instead of court-marshalling a soldier for stealing a dead soldier's belongings, he made him dig the soldier's grave with his bare hands.

I want to tell this story because it represents so many families' experiences during the war. The United States was unprepared when Pearl Harbor was attacked, causing an immediate political, psychological, and economic shift and having a profound effect on family life. Families were separated in order to fight to protect America's way of life. For example, my grandmother was one of five million "war widows" raising children alone. Anxiety, uncertainty, and fear, due to the separation from fathers and sons, had a profound effect. Someone warned my grandfather on his return that he wouldn't recognize my grandmother, as her hair had turned completely white and she had aged dramatically during his absence.

Through a galvanized effort by the vast majority of its citizens, the United States was able to contribute to a World War II victory. Sacrifices and death permeated the fabric of this country and were felt for years. However, so many individuals have benefitted from the efforts of millions of people to this day. My grandfather, Lt. Col. James Francis Greene, and his wife, Ann Smith Greene, were grateful to have been able to contribute to the challenges of their day to better the lives of future generations.

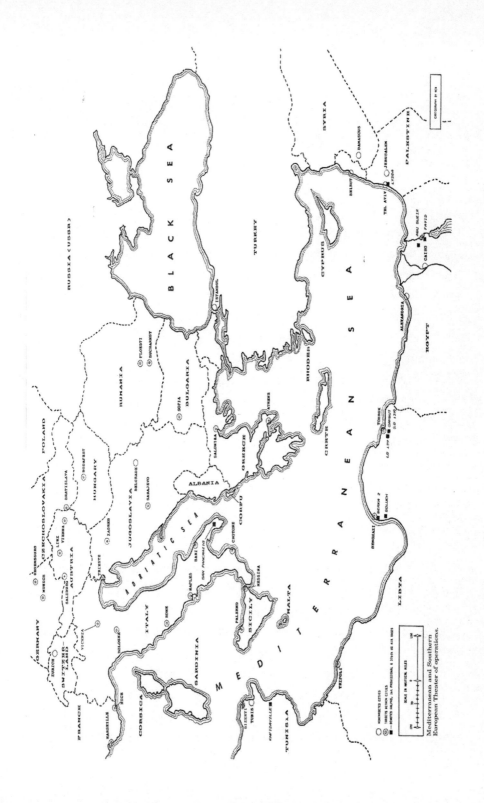

Mediterranean and Southern
European Theater of operations.

Chapter 1
Above Reproach

Like the British soldier in Rudyard Kipling's poem, *Mandalay*, Jim Greene wanted to be shipped somewhere east of the Suez Canal in Egypt, "where the best is like the worst." He was ready to explore and conquer the world after graduating from college in 1922 and he thought the military would be his ticket. Instead, it took 20 years and World War II to realize his dream of adventure. During the interim, he used his talents in his hometown of Washington, D.C. and developed the skills needed later in his life.

His early years, though privileged, began with his father's tragic suicide. His mother, Ellen Marbury Beale Greene, decided to give birth at her well-appointed brick home in the country in Northern Virginia. She had recently purchased the farm from her Marbury relatives who had taken her in after her parents' deaths. She relished roaming around the grounds and was soothed by the sounds of nature and the cooler breezes. Summers in Washington, D.C. were hot and abundant with germ carrying insects from the ship traffic and unsanitary conditions at the Georgetown wharf, the largest on the eastern seaboard. Ellen chose to retreat to her country home when her baby was due.

As his mother had wished, James Francis Greene was born at Spring Hill Farm, in Hamilton, VA, on September 17, 1899. Ellen recuperated in the Catoctin mountains and enjoyed the rich hues of the fall hillside. Four weeks later, she had not received word of her husband's travel plans so she took her newborn son and his older brother, Albert, back to their home in the Georgetown neighborhood of Washington, D.C. Meanwhile, her husband, Albert Greene, a lawyer in New York City, took the train to Hamilton, a hamlet located 45 miles west of Washington, D.C., to visit his family and meet his new son. Despondent over his mounting gambling debts and arriving at an empty house, he took a rifle out of the gun closet, walked to the fenced pasture, and shot himself, making it appear to be an accident.

Ellen, a young widow at age 25, laid her husband to rest near other beloved family members in the Georgetown neighborhood burial grounds, Oak Hill Cemetery, in Washington, D.C. She often walked through the tree canopied cemetery and visited the many graves of her relatives. Her father, a respected surgeon in Washington, D.C. died when she was 10; her mother died when she was 19. Afterwards, Ellen and her three younger siblings went to live with their mother's two older maiden aunts. They had helped raise Ellen's mother and now they cared for the younger children and gave Ellen much support at this sad time.

Ellen confronted her widowhood with grace and fortitude. She welcomed each day with gratitude for her healthy sons, Albert and Jim. Raising them gave her purpose and pleasure.

But she still mourned her husband's death. Upon returning to her farm the following spring, she expressed her grief by writing this poem:

How strange to think you are dead,
Now that the spring mice waken here.
The wind flows in its woodland bed,
The pink arbutus trailing near.
The air sweet of song of bird.
With lilting leaf, and gurgling hill,
Every blade of grass has stirred.
And only you are still so still.
The eager heart that held no care,
The wandering feet that loved to stray,
Those eyes which saw God's world so fair,
Alas they come not back with May!
Was it indeed because you knew,
How short the time you might not waste
Finding the hours all too few
You quaffed life's cup in joyous haste?
With gay distain you put it by
Leaving the loss of us to drain

And still the hillside where you lie
Is starred with daffodil again.

Ellen's second child, James Francis Greene, Francis as Jim was known as a child, had a sweet disposition and showed compassion for others. He began his life-long practice of writing notes to special people as a young boy. When he was four, he sent the following note to his aunt in South Carolina:

Dear Auntie Florence,

If you are a little better, I asked God to make you well. Maybe that made you well.

James Francis Greene

When Francis was seven, his mother married Walter Peter, an older family friend who was an architect in Washington, D.C. Walter was a kind gentleman and a respected businessman. He was a supportive stepfather and an important role model to Francis. When the newlyweds went on their honeymoon, Francis was sad but appreciated the postcard his mother sent to him. His early love of storytelling, along with his talent for creating imaginary bears and bear drawings, appeared in his response to his mother.

Dear Mother,

I am real sorry you went away. It is really hot. Penna does not like the heat. He is a polar bear. I got the postcard you sent me. Thank you for it. All the bears send their love.

Francis Greene

Francis seemed to develop a sense of knowing right from wrong, and to realize the benefit of telling the truth at a young age. He confessed in a note to his mother, "I did not take an apple to school after all so will eat it when I get home." Being honest was reinforced and paid dividends throughout his life.

Francis's extended family, including his uncle and his daughters, enhanced his life. Ellen's younger brother, Dr. Robert Beale, chose their father's profession and settled in the same neighborhood with his wife, Sophie. They had three daughters who doted on their cousin and nicknamed him "Hanny." The families celebrated all special occasions and spent their summers together at Rehoboth Beach, Delaware. Hanny took to the sand and sun and spent hours making sand sculptures for his cousins and playing in the ocean.

Their visits to Spring Hill Farm in the mountains provided a different set of outdoor experiences. Horseback riding, fishing in the creek, and hiking in the woods were favorite pastimes. Hanny became proficient with a shotgun by shooting squirrels and rabbits. He told stories to his cousins and other younger children. He even shared his imaginary tales with his dog and the farm animals. Occasionally, he wrote a story for his mother, an aunt or another important adult in his life. His stories usually were about his ever-present bears and other animals that were compatible with the setting, whether the beach, the mountains or the city.

One rainy summer afternoon, his mother assumed the role of storyteller. Hanny and his cousins were having a pillow fight when someone threw a chair cushion. The seam ripped, and several letters written during the Civil War fell out. "Aunt Ellen, Aunt Ellen, look what we found!" shouted the girls. The letters had been written by her father during the Civil War and hastily sewn into the chair cushion by members of the family because they feared being arrested as Southern sympathizers.

She proceeded to tell the children about their grandfather's escapade. Ellen's father, James Beale, as a rebellious teenager, ran off and joined a Confederate unit at the age of 16, much to the chagrin of his father, who served in the United States government as the Sergeant of Arms of the U.S. Congress and other positions with President Lincoln. During the war, many people were arrested in Washington, D.C. for being Southern sympathizers; and therefore, they had to be very careful about communications from family and friends fighting for the Confederacy. Along with many local families and friends, the

Beales were divided in their allegiances, partly due to their family loyalties. James returned safely after the war and entered medical school.

Ellen explained that her father chose a career in medicine after seeing the injuries and death on the battlefield. She emphasized that one can make a dangerous choice, but once in that position, you have to do the best you can, in some cases to protect your life and that of others. She explained that a person could make a mistake, especially a teenager, learn from the experience, and then mature into a well-respected contributing member of society. However, a decision may have a serious impact on our families.

Ellen also told them that Hanny's paternal grandfather served on the Union side as an engineer on the *Susquehanna* with U.S. Navy Atlantic blockading squadron during the war. Later, his grandfather, Albert S. Greene, travelled around the world serving on many ships with the Navy. Hanny inherited a sense of fearlessness and adventure from both sides of his family.

From a young age, he developed an allegiance to the United States, established and defended by his ancestors since the Revolutionary War.

During Hanny's childhood, Georgetown was a small sophisticated community with the personality of a southern town. World leaders, lawyers, and politicians lived in the neighborhood throughout the year. The houses were close together. Neighbors socialized often in the evenings and during the weekends. Political party affiliations took a backseat to the issues of the day. A devotion to building the future of the country still carried over from the early days of the young republic. The children heard a clear message that they were called to be responsible citizens and serve others. Many members of the family became teachers, lawyers, doctors, ministers, or served in the military.

Hanny and his friends liked to ride their bikes down to the docks and watch the ships unload their cargo. The Georgetown port on the Potomac River played a major role in the development of the eastern seaboard. Tobacco, sugar, timber, Appalachian coal, and New England ice were moved through the port. Sailors from distant places intrigued Hanny, and piqued his interest in what lay beyond Georgetown.

The boys liked to cast a line in the Potomac River or the Chesapeake and Potomac Canal.

In the early part of the 20th century, it was easy for the youngsters to find a vacant lot to play baseball. It became Hanny's favorite sport. He and his brother, Albert, occasionally were treated to a day at Glen Echo Park. They practiced at the shooting gallery and rode the Gyroplane and later, the Derby Racer.

When Hanny was nine, his mother and Walter Peter, his stepfather, had a son together and named him Walter, Jr. Hanny loved his little brother, and they stayed close until Hanny's death.

Hanny attended St. Albans Boys Preparatory School and the Cathedral School, located just north of Georgetown. He struggled with academics, so after eighth grade he transferred to a public high school, McKinley Manual Training. Although physical activity and drawing were his lifelong passions, he appreciated the importance of an education as a result of growing up in a family that valued learning.

During his junior year in high school, it was recommended that Hanny consider attending Virginia Military Institute, a military college in Lexington, VA. His uncle, Garden Stuart, who graduated in 1897 and became a doctor, felt that VMI's structure would be beneficial in giving him some direction, possibly in the military. When his principal completed the paperwork for Hanny's application, his comments described Hanny's poor scholarship preparation and mediocre intellectual promise. However, the principal did praise his seriousness of effort and noted that Hanny's character was above reproach.

Hanny was accepted to VMI and matriculated in September 1917, just shy of his 18th birthday, with his best childhood friend, Sam Syme. There were 579 men in barracks, with about 300 new cadets due to an increased need for Army officers during World War I. Superintendent Nichols' remarks at the beginning of the year shaped Hanny's life and endeared him to VMI.

"The stand you take is the stand you make. You rise and fall on your own achievements! Honor. Character. Determination. No VMI man is a quitter. Be afraid of nothing that walks God's green earth except to do wrong!"

Although Jimmy, as he became known at VMI, found the academics very challenging, he did find time to get into trouble during his freshman year or "rat year," as it is known at VMI. He wasn't happy that he couldn't be with his family for Christmas and got into a bit of mischief by triggering an explosion that caused quite some damage to the chemistry lab.

Correspondence from his mother to the superintendent expressed her embarrassment and disappointment upon receiving a bill for the damages.

My dear General Nichols,

Your communication just received in regard to my son, J.F. Greene, was a great shock to me. Francis has always been such a good boy! I have sent a telegram and also a letter that I hope will bring him to his senses. Please find enclosed a check for $396 (more than a semester's tuition) in payment of the enclosed bill. I sincerely trust that Francis will give no further cause for complaint.

Very truly yours,
Ellen Beale Peter

Due to the war in Europe, the United States Army announced that the quota assigned for the ROTC at the Institute was raised from 108 to 300 because of the superior training received at VMI. Jimmy was selected to attend officers' training camp at Plattsburgh, N.Y. in 1918. The Plattsburgh camp was comprised of men of high standing in business, professional and social affairs who were willing to make personal sacrifices for the country's common good. American officers trained there made beneficial use of lessons taught as it grounded a large number of intelligent Americans in the rudiments of warfare.

With his determined gray eyes and fair complexion, this 5-foot 6-inch teenager began his first military participation on June 3, 1918, after completing one year at VMI. During his time in the Students Corps, Jim learned much about infantry warfare and improved his riflery skills. He particularly enjoyed his time on horseback in the cavalry. However, peace broke out before Jim saw action, as the Armistice was signed on November 11, 1918, ending the need for a large infantry and the cadets' brief stint in the military. Jim was honorably discharged on December 10, 1918, after serving six months. He returned to VMI, and due to a case of mumps, fell behind in his schoolwork.

For the first 81 years at the Institute, students didn't leave campus for their winter break but stayed in the barracks over the holidays. Dress parade was held on Christmas day. However, at the suggestion of General John J. Pershing, a visiting World War I military leader, an eight-day Christmas furlough was instituted in 1920. However, those who were deficient in any subject or had over 35 demerits could not leave barracks. Consequently, Jim was not able to leave for Christmas that year due to his grades.

Earlier that year, Jimmy's academic challenges had also prevented him from attending his aunt's funeral in May at Troy, NY. General Edward W. Nichols stated his decision in a telegram to Ellen: "It will jeopardize Jimmy's ability to pass his exams." Jim was disappointed because family was so important to him. However, staying at school proved insufficient for him to pass. General Nichols notified Jim and his mother that he would be required to repeat his third year.

After a year of civil engineering, Jim decided a liberal arts course of study would better fit him for the world's challenges. During his college years, he excelled in the military aspect of VMI, played baseball, and ran track. Although it was necessary for him to concentrate on his school work and military responsibilities, he used his artistic talents on the staff of the yearbook, *The Bomb*. His senior quote sums up his desire to travel in far off places. "Send me somewhere east of Suez, where the best is like the worst." The line was from one of Jim's favorite authors, Rudyard Kipling's poem, *Mandalay*.

*Ship me somewhere east of Suez, where the best is like the worst, Where there aren't no Ten Commandments and a man can raise a thirst; For the temple bells are callin', and it's there that I would be—
By the old Moulmein Pagoda, looking lazy at the sea.*

Rudyard Kipling, a well-known British author and poet, spent seven years in India. He wrote the poem in 1890 about Mandalay, the sometime capital of Burma, now Myanmar, having been struck by the beauty of the Burmese women during an unexpected stop. Kipling, at age 24, was traveling with two friends from Calcutta to Japan, and on to San Francisco, crossing the United States before returning to England.

Jim's academic challenges gave him an opportunity to develop his perseverance. Although he was near the bottom of his class, Jim finally graduated after five years with a Bachelor of Arts in History on June 18, 1922. He was remembered by his classmates for being a friend to all.

After graduation, Jim reported to Army Reserve duty at Fort Meade, MD. He served in the Officers Reserve Corps for six weeks and realized, although he would have liked to enter the military, it wasn't an option at this time. The bloodshed and destruction of World War I led to widespread opposition to further military involvement in foreign conflicts. Antimilitarism set in and Congress drastically cut the size of the military to 150,000.

Jim moved back to Georgetown and lived with his mother, step-father, and little brother, Walter, in a large brick home on N Street, within walking distance to other family homes, Oak Hill cemetery, and their favorite watering hole, Martin's Tavern. He raised a few pints with his large extended family and many friends in the Washington, D.C. area and those who visited from places like Richmond, Baltimore, Pittsburgh, and Philadelphia.

Jim was living a comfortable and pleasant life, staying in touch with and visiting his college friends. He liked attending professional sporting events, particularly football and baseball and an occasional boxing match. His cousins called on him to escort them and their friends to social functions when necessary. It would take him a few years to find a profession where he could use his drawing talent and communication skills. He eventually found his niche in advertising. After spending several years settling into his career, he began to contemplate finding a life's companion.

Chapter 2
The Only Girl

After VMI, Jim got a job working for the telephone company for a couple of years until his best friend, Sam Syme, graduated from Harvard Law School. In celebration, they took off for Europe. They boarded a ship in the New York City harbor and spent two weeks playing cards, reading and engaging in "bull sessions" with the other passengers while they crossed the Atlantic toward England. A favorite pastime was watching huge fish swim alongside the ship for miles and miles and following the whales and their waterspouts, while getting sunburned and nursing cold beers.

By 1924, London had recovered from World War I and prosperity was evident. The nightclubs, jazz clubs and cocktail bars flourished, giving an energetic atmosphere for two traveling young men. During the day, Jim and Sam walked the streets, admired the architecture, and visited the famous sites and museums.

After a week, they took the train to Paris, reestablished after the war as a capital of art, music, literature and cinema. The artistic environment and low prices attracted writers and artists from around the world such as Pablo Picasso, Salvador Dali, Ernest Hemingway, James Joyce, and Josephine Baker. In addition to visiting historical sites and listening to different types of music, they also encountered many languages of diverse cultures. After getting a taste of the beauty and culture of the much older cities of London and Paris and vowing to continue to travel in the future, Sam and Jim returned to the U.S. to establish careers.

Upon arrival in Washington, D.C., Sam began his career in law while Jim figured out a way to use his artistic ability and people skills. He went to work in advertising where he would help sell the new merchandise being produced in the years after World War I. A few well-known items invented in the 1920s and still used today include the washing machine, the vacuum cleaner, the electric blender, the radio, and smaller product such as frozen foods, the band-aid, and the electric razor. It was a time when advertising was becoming a major factor in the economy, as the U.S. was producing lots of consumer goods and looking for creative ways to market them. Jim contacted his large circle of friends in the mid-Atlantic region whom he felt could benefit from his services.

After five years of developing his talents, Jim co-founded Walton-Hoke, a commercial art firm in Washington, D.C. and Baltimore. Jim focused on developing the agency, which required many road trips to see clients in places like Pittsburgh, Philadelphia, and New York. He learned to listen to his clients and convey their message in drawings illustrating use of their products.

After four years of long hours and traveling many miles for work, Jim met Ann Fontaine Smith during the summer of 1928 at a friend's wedding. She was visiting her parents in Washington, D.C. during summer break from her teaching position in Staunton, Virginia. The two found common interests in literature and poetry. As an English major in college, Ann studied the classics with a fondness for Shakespeare. Like Jim's mother, she enjoyed writing poetry.

Jim appreciated her writing ability and she admired his drawing talent. Jim had majored in history and particularly liked reading about distant lands and other cultures. They shared an understanding of American history, learned mostly from family discussions, and kept abreast of world events.

During her summer months in Washington, D.C., they often packed a picnic and took drives out in the country. Jim got a taste of Ann's cooking skills and she learned of his love of animals and plants, acquired from his summers spent in the country. One weekend they drove to Rehoboth Beach to visit Jim's cousins and found that they both shared an appreciation for tranquility at the seashore and warm weather.

Also, that summer Ann and Jim both had fun watching competitive sporting events and attended a few professional football and baseball games. Ann played basketball while Jim played baseball during their college days.

After a fun-filled summer, Ann returned for the new school year. She taught at Stuart Hall, a private girls' school, since her graduation from Longwood College in 1920. Ann and Jim continued their courtship through written correspondence and a few visits. Jim reiterated his affection in his first letter, "And just when I'd decided if there ever had been 'the only girl' and that she must have stepped out with someone else, along comes Ann, and hope springs eternal." He often enlivened the letters with drawings and developed some of his animal stories at this time.

In October of that year, Jim consoled Ann during her bout with a sore throat, a common affliction for a teacher with young students. After her recovery and with much anticipation, he was ready to escort Ann to a football game weekend at VMI in Lexington. He could hardly wait. "Cut the guide ropes, boys – let's go! I'm set to ride and waiting for the gun." He set off for a fall weekend drive from the big city, through the colorful Shenandoah Valley.

After several changes of weekend plans, Jim arrived in Staunton early on a Saturday morning. He warned Ann, "This will be the first time I ever dragged a girl to a VMI game so tell me how to behave, and above all things, don't get excited. Be cool like me." They watched the game and had dinner with Jim's best friend, Sam, and his fiancé, Martha. They had a wonderful time and their weekend together confirmed their thoughts about one another after being apart for a few months, and strengthened their emotional connection.

Jim struggled to compose letters to Ann.

"Your letters are beautiful and make mine seem so poor by contrast. I want to say just lots of things and write just as I think, but I'm not in a position to back anything up and it wouldn't be shooting square with you. I want to see you again as soon as possible. I hope and pray you won't fall for someone else.

"I reckon now you know I'm dumb, but I know you are a straight thinker and square as they make 'em so maybe you'll realize how I feel and always remember if you do have a little love to send me it is returned a hundred times."

During that fall, Jim attended many weddings. On the weekend of November 17, he headed to Richmond for a VMI classmate's wedding. Before Sam and Martha's wedding, he and Sam enjoyed one last bachelor outing, drank lots of champagne, and recuperated driving back in the warm sun.

Jim worked long hours while waiting for Ann's Thanksgiving visit. "I'm most afraid to meet you for fear I'll do something foolish like trip over my own feet in the excitement, but you'll have to excuse me, remembering my inexperience and youth."

Jim met Ann's parents and spent time with her family during the holiday break. Mr. and Mrs. Smith were staying with Ann's sister, Mary, and her husband, Julian, after their father's heart attack. Their siblings, Emma and Witcher, drove from Danville, Virginia, to join them for Thanksgiving. Ann's family got to know Jim and he got to know the extended Smith family while playing a few hands of bridge.

During this visit, Jim's friend, Eddie Brown, met Ann. Eddie expressed interest in her, causing Jim to feel a little competition. Jim felt a compliment was in order to address a potential rival, as he saw it, so he wrote Ann, "Gee, but you have pretty eyes and cute little ankles and I like the way you talk... When is your train arriving for Christmas break?"

While waiting for Christmas, Jim helped his friend, Sam, prepare and celebrate his and Martha's wedding. As a groomsman, he wanted to make sure the couple got off to a good start with all the usual pranks. Sam and Martha were married on December 14th and the newlyweds snuck away without getting showered with rice, so a few friends decorated their house on their return from their honeymoon.

After he and Ann spent the winter break together, Jim attempted to describe his feelings to Ann:

"Ann, dear I can't write much cause I'm too busy thinking about your pretty brown eyes and nice red cheeks and how quick the Christmas holidays pass. First, I think about you and I am very happy then I remember you're gone and there's a terrible reaction.

Of course, I'm still as determined as ever that I'll never bother about any girl but that doesn't include thinking about you, dreaming about you, wishing for you and feeling miserable now that you've left. I suppose you were met in Staunton.

Ann, sweetheart, we've just got to see each other again soon. Why bother about work anyhow? I never did approve of it.

Would you still be glad to see me? I'll write again tomorrow so good night pretty… love, Jimmy."

After Ann's return to her teaching position in Staunton, Jim stayed in touch with the Smith family, which gave everybody a chance to get better acquainted. He learned that the company for which Mr. Smith had worked granted him leave to convalesce, which was a relief to all. It meant that they would be staying in Washington, D.C. for the time being. Jim took the Smiths out for a few Sunday afternoon drives. One excursion took them to visit their mutual friends, Sam and Martha, in their new home; another outing was a trip to Spring Hill Farm.

As the weather turned cold, Jim thought about sitting in front of a big open fire with Ann. "…dreams do come true sometimes and the present I'll dream of…" he wrote. The dream came true. A few weeks later, Ann was able to hitch a ride home for the weekend.

The surprise visit didn't go well because Jim didn't like the man who drove Ann to Washington, D.C., moreover, she had a few commitments with friends. He was worried that Ann might be interested in the other fellow, and Jim wanted to spend more time with her. Jim wrote: "Ann sweetheart, forgive me for being so disagreeable while you were here. I'm peculiar, I just don't seem to really appreciate all you really do when you are here. I hated myself, the man you were with, and everything except you, and now I feel mean and lonely and know I deserve to feel that way."

Ann made plans to take the mail train to Washington, D.C., for a Valentine's Day weekend. Ann asked Jim if she could hug him at the train station and his response, "So long as too many of your large-size admirers aren't present to watch me reciprocate." Their time together during this visit made up for the previous disappointing weekend.

Ann shared that she was invited to Hawaii for the summer. Jim's response, "If you decide to go to Hawaii, let me know in time to get a ticket on the same boat." On a realistic note, he countered with plans in Washington, D.C. for summer drives in the evening, or canoeing on the Potomac River, or a trip to Glen Echo for a ride on the roller coaster.

To pass the time until Ann's next visit, Jim spent long hours at work. He lamented that one windy day a big plate glass window fell out of the Press Building and hit his new automobile. He writes, "Their insurance company is trying to sneak out of paying for the damage by saying their insurance only reaches to the curb." Unfortunately, he learned that his insurance was only for fire and theft and being hit by someone else. He ended up having to pay for the damage.

When Jim had a night off, he often visited with Martha and Sam and listened to the fights on the radio when they couldn't find a fourth for bridge. He also spent time with his cousins, filling in as an escort to formal social gatherings for absentee husbands.

Meanwhile, Ann enjoyed an active social life in Staunton with friends and colleagues. She went on a few dates, but Jim was her priority. She contacted a friend at Arlington Hall in Washington, D.C. about a teaching prospect for the fall. Her friend, Carrie, set up an interview with the school's President.

One Saturday night, Jim's friends, Jack White and Eddie, came to town and drank all his liquor. Jim reported: "There's a great beverage shortage in this town due to this new law giving bootleggers a $10,000 fine and five years. The price of drinks has doubled and until the price of police protection has been adjusted the stuff is difficult to get except by prominent people like cabinet members and congressmen who are known not to be federal agents."

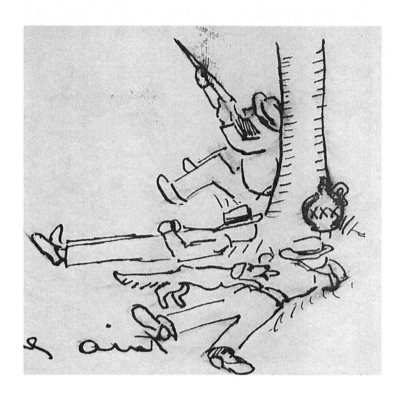

His boredom waiting for Ann's return made him contemplate other ways of making a living and joked to Ann, "Even the Mexican revolution is going on the blink when I had started to delve into the possibility of smuggling arms to the revolutionists. This I thought would be a pleasant and profitable posture, giving as much excitement as bootlegging but not quite so plebian."

Meanwhile, spring break was full of activity for Ann. She interviewed at Arlington Hall and looked into possible living arrangements. Jim took her to meet his scrutinizing cousins. He shared their comments, "The Beales are crazy about you. All of them thought you were pretty and attractive. Liz (Leahy) added to the general praise by saying, 'She has lots of sense, too.' And they all marveled that I, alone and unaided, had found such a divine creature and enticed her into my automobile. (I think they all like me but really don't appreciate my remarkable ability – ahem!)"

After a wave of happy times, Jim came up short on several fronts. A client wasn't pleased with his work; a cop gave him a parking ticket; his car wouldn't start because of a clogged gas line; and his resulting irritation caused a filling to fall out of his tooth! And like many other Americans, Jim was feeling the effects at work from the beginning of the Great Depression. As a result, he needed to be at the office for more hours, cutting into his socializing and plans with Ann. Most importantly, he came to realize how much Ann meant to him.

In Staunton, Ann was busy with her students and thinking about her future teaching plans. She was offered a position at Arlington Hall and contemplated leaving Stuart Hall after eight years. She decided to accept the offer, resigned her current position, and planned a move to Washington, D.C. at the end of the school year.

Jim was ecstatic but still a little worried Ann might fall for another guy. He warns her, "It must be awfully pretty in the country now and this time of the year it's not safe to leave you alone with all that competition down there. Just remember if anybody says sweet things to you, I'm just thinking lots sweeter ones about you and anyway don't believe all these boys tell you as you can't trust them at this time of year anyhow."

Ann's potential move to Washington, D.C. was a cause of ongoing celebration. Jim filled the time while he waited for her arrival. He got together with his friends, Eddie and Jack, in the countryside where they shot a few red squirrels and basked in a sun-filled weekend. They stopped and played poker with Martha and Sam on the way home. The next day, he drove to Baltimore to share the good news with his friend, Goldie. After a trip to VMI as a government inspection representative and a visit with Ann, he stopped to share his good news with his VMI roommate, Nat Pendleton.

Jim's friends, Rip and Goldie, came in from Baltimore and they hoisted a few and said good-bye to his roommate and good friend, Jack, who was moving to New York for a new job. "Eddie and I are the only two bachelors that amount to anything in town." Jim was becoming concerned that he would be the only member of the bachelor's club.

Jim made his last visit to see Ann in Staunton in early May. After a wonderful time together, Jim had to change a flat tire on the way home. Nobody paused to help, but a couple of dogs in a nearby farmhouse serenaded him. He arrived home at 2:31 a.m. and sent a telegram to let Ann know he made it safely.

His family, particularly his little brother, continued to praise his choice in a girlfriend. His cousins looked forward to hearing about Ann and having her in Washington, D.C. On the other hand, his mother thought Ann was too good for him, and that she should find a better suitor. He relayed those sentiments to Ann, "Mother thinks the handkerchiefs that you embroidered for her are beautiful and can't understand why such a bright little girl who could do something like that should waste time on me. Your position is certainly strong with my family." As Jim was growing more enamored with Ann, he agreed with his mother that perhaps she would think he wasn't good enough for her.

Jim was adjusting to this next phase of life in which his family and friends were getting married and having children. He commented about his new role as an uncle to Albert's child. He was also asked to be the godfather for his cousin, Liz Beale Leahy's daughter, Louise. His remark to this new responsibility, "Poor Kid."

As the time drew closer for Ann's move to Washington, D.C., Jim was looking forward to verbalizing feelings that he hadn't thought were conveyed accurately in his letters. He was anticipating the freedom from short visits with her, due to the distance between them. Jim felt that their ease in talking and seeing each other would help alleviate his concern about other potential suitors.

Ann finished her responsibilities at Stuart Hall and in Staunton and readied for the next chapter in her life. At the last minute before her move, Jim had to go to Philadelphia to see a client so he couldn't meet Ann's train. He lamented in his last letter to Staunton, "I feel like I'd run a two-mile race and just at the finish line had somebody tell me it was changed to a marathon."

Jim was not the only person happy that Ann moved to Washington, D.C. Her sister, Mary, and brother-in-law, Julian, were pleased to have her live with them. Although she immediately began preparation for her teaching responsibilities at Arlington Hall in the fall, their parents, who also were living with Mary and Julian, enjoyed having Ann as a fourth at the bridge table when Julian was away on business and she wasn't out with Jim.

Ann's first semester in her new school went by quickly. Ann and Jim were grateful to have jobs as the Depression descended upon the country. Fortunately, Jim had lived at home for much of the last seven years and squirreled away a little savings as his business grew.

Ann and another teacher rented rooms and lived in a large home with a widow. She had worked and saved for the past nine years. There was no Social Security, so they knew about saving for rainy days and the future.

Both families and their wide circle of friends were elated when Ann and Jim became engaged on Ann's birthday, December 14, 1929. Planning began for an August wedding before school resumed from summer break. Ann was appreciative that her mother and sister were available to attend to the details of the nuptials while she continued with her teaching responsibilities. Their marriage celebration took place at Christ Episcopal Church, Georgetown, on August 23, 1930. Jim's family had worshipped there since its founding in 1817. His cousin, Rev. Albert Rhett Stuart, presided at the marriage. He later became the Bishop of Georgia and was very supportive of civil rights and integration during the 1960s.

Ann's cousin, Nancy Astor, who lived in England, gave them tickets to travel and visit her for a wedding present. They took the train to New York City, boarded a ship in the harbor, and sailed to Plymouth, England. Nancy took them on a weeklong tour to London and her estate, Cliveden, before returning them to Plymouth for their trip back to the United States.

Ann returned to set up housekeeping in their new home. Since she'd rented a room in Staunton, running a household was a new adventure for her. The two-story brick and sided house with a small yard was in a Chevy Chase neighborhood where the sidewalks were framed with trees. It was an adequate three-bedroom home for a young family in a Washington, D.C. suburb, within walking distance to area schools.

Once she mastered household management, Ann found herself preparing for motherhood. She was pregnant within nine months of their marriage and Jimmy, Jr. was born on February 12, 1932. Billy was born 22 months later on December 11, 1933. Ann was quite busy with two active boys.

Jim continued to travel to see clients, and helped keep the business solvent during trying economic times. He found time to serve as president of the Washington, D.C. Chapter of the V.M.I. Alumni Association and invited his fellow alumnus and friend, then Colonel George Marshall, to speak. Marshall accepted and addressed the group on May 15, 1933, sharing his thoughts on the happenings in Europe. Jim kept abreast of military involvement around the world through correspondence with family and friends.

Ann's father and his cousin Nancy Astor, who still lived in England, continued to correspond as Hitler's dream of conquering and dominating Europe became a reality. Edgar Smith shared his thoughts with Nancy in regards to a Saturday Evening Post article on March 16, 1939.

"I am glad that you endorsed the appeasement policy of the Prime Minister (Neville Chamberlain), and while I regretted the necessity of compromise, under the circumstances, I could see no alternative. War is horrible! And any means, short of cowardice and dishonor justify its being averted, or even postponed. My thirty years' connection with the Imperial Tobacco Company and frequent visits to England give me a fair conception of the British thought, and I am sure the large majority of the people will approve of his policy.

"However, it seems from recent events that Hitler's dream of a Drang Nach Osten (German National Movement), as outlined in Mein Kampf is to become reality, and he has set out to conquer and to dominate all of Europe, and defy Democracies. Unless our civilization is to be destroyed, it would seem that the final show-down will have to come soon, and the real Armageddon still to be fought. Though the policy of America in recent years has seemed pusillanimous to me, when the real crisis comes, I feel sure that America will assert itself and be found on the side of the French and English as before.

"I recently viewed the portrait of your mother, which was donated to Greensboro College last spring. It was a beautiful picture, and a striking likeness as I remember her in the days of my youth."

Nancy's letter of September 15, 1940 assures Edgar that in spite of the Blitzkrieg, all was well with her family.

"All my boys are in the Services, and all well and safe I am grateful to say, or as safe as anyone else over here just now!! Bobbie is in the Home Guard and is in the very front line in the South East, Bill is in the Navy and has been stationed in Egypt for twelve months last May, David is in the Marines, at present stationed at Portsmouth having a pretty hot time, and recently a really miraculous escape, and the two youngest are in a Reconnaissance Unit recruited from the Guards – their work is secret and highly dangerous, but they care nothing as long as they are together. They are very much of an age, and have always been like twins, so life's troubles and pleasures count very little to them so long as they are shared. All except Bill get home occasionally, but leave is very scarce with the invasion pending.

We have a Canadian Red Cross hospital erected on the grounds here, and this keeps us pretty occupied. At present there are about 300 patients, this is only half its complement.

London is having a hard time now, but the people are magnificent. The problem of dealing with the homeless is pretty acute, but it is amazing how things work themselves out as we go along. The experience of our little parlor maid in London is typical. A couple of nights ago she was in a shelter with her invalid mother when a bomb fell on it, killing half the people, and also bursting the water main, with the result that the place was flooded in a few minutes and the rescuers had a great deal of trouble getting them out at all. They had not been long on the surface, when another siren sounded and they were put into another shelter, when they got out of that about luncheon time, they found out that the block of flats in which they lived had been struck by a bomb, rendering the whole place uninhabitable for the time being anyway, so they were homeless. Of course, we are glad to have them in our house, so they are better off than most, but it is a typical situation in which thousands of Londoners have found themselves in the past week.

Although the people do not like the idea of Buckingham Palace having been hit, because of what it stands for – in a way I think it is a good thing, as the people will feel how very true is the saying, 'We are all in this together.'

I do know how you feel about America's attitude to the whole situation but they are perhaps doing as much as they can in sending material, and that is certainly the most important thing at the moment. The rejoicing over our exchange of bases and warships here has been very great. For myself I am sure it is the first step in a great new era for mankind. If only America and the British Empire can unite their purpose and their plans for righteous government the world over, we shall win through. Perhaps the actual battle is ours, I don't know, but if America has a place to take in the fighting line, she will have to take it, whether she likes it or not. His ways are not always ours.

If… passes England send me some gum or molasses candy."

In the United States peacetime life continued for two years after the war began in Europe. For the Greenes, a welcome addition to the family occurred when baby Ann was born on February 20, 1941. Jim was enamored with a daughter after growing up with two brothers and having two sons. At the age of 41, he felt blessed to have a little girl in the family. Jim thought she was the most beautiful child and relished watching her grow.

The advertising agency survived the 1930s and was flourishing when Pearl Harbor was bombed on December 7, 1941. The attack had a monumental impact on the Greene family's immediate future. When the United States entered the war, the family faced difficult decisions. The choices tested Ann's and Jim's character and resolve, and their commitment to each other and to their country.

Chapter 3
Called to Serve

Ten-year-old Jimmy and eight-year-old Billy stood at attention with their gloved hands saluting military and political leaders as they paraded in the nation's Capital. The boys' homemade dark gray, matching Army uniforms and hats kept them warm on this chilly December day in 1941. Jimmy's straight brown hair topped his cherubic face. His inquisitive light eyes and natural smile revealed contentment and he appeared to be pondering the effects of this momentous event. Billy's sad demeanor showed in his scowl and downturned mouth. He looked at much of life as an unpleasant challenge to confront or a disappointment to overcome. Ann, their petite mother, with brown curly hair and stern brown eyes, sat erect as she watched her boys. She was a strict former teacher and her high expectations permeated their lives.

The parade welcomed British Prime Minister Winston Churchill to Washington, D.C. shortly after the bombings at Pearl Harbor on December 7th. The Prime Minister and President Franklin Roosevelt met to discuss how Britain and the United States could best coordinate a strategy in the wake of Japan's recent attack. The assault on the American Navy galvanized the country.

After the parade, the boys and their parents joined their relatives for one of their frequent family gatherings. The Marshall girls were enjoying their holiday and always had fun with their Greene cousins. Jim Greene and Florence Beale Marshall grew up as close as siblings and still enjoyed spending time together and would continue to throughout their lives.

Billy, a ringleader, shouted to his cousins at the gathering, "Let's go outside and play kick the can."

A loud response from the others followed, "Yeah!" A scurry of activity unfolded as the cousins grabbed their hats, coats and mittens and headed outdoors. It didn't take long for the neighborhood children to join the fun. The friends spent the afternoon teasing each other and playing games.

Florence, with energetic brown eyes and a sharp wit, orchestrated the activities of the day. Ann followed her into the kitchen to prepare dinner and set the table. Their baby daughters toddled around, pulling up on the kitchen cabinets and making noise with the utensils and pots and pans. Florence shared a compliment. "Ann, your sewing is magnificent. The boys looked adorable standing at attention in their uniforms while the bands marched by."

"Thank you! That was quite a welcome for Mr. Churchill. The music kept me from feeling so cold. The Bethesda-Chevy Chase High School band played an enthusiastic rendition of the Star Spangled Banner while passing in front of us."

Florence responded as she handed Ann a mug, "It was great to see so many supportive, patriotic people. How about some hot cider?" Dick Marshall, Florence's husband, walked into the kitchen and handed Florence a bourbon and water.

The men fixed themselves a drink and headed into the living room. Dick, a tall man, with a commanding presence, strode to his favorite chair. He commented as he looked at Jim, "I guess some of us will get a second chance to serve in a war."

Jim, all of his 5'6", trim 145 pounds, took several steps to cross the large foyer. His receding brown hair and serious gray eyes hid his fun-loving, compassionate personality. He responded, "Can I remember what I learned 20 years ago?"

Dick said, "If they need me, it will certainly be a different type of legal work than I'm doing now."

Jim joked, "I don't think they need advertising expertise."

Dick answered, "You have other talents. You can get the boys in shape."

Jim started thinking realistically, "That's an idea. I can help train the troops at Fort Meade or Fort Myer. I became pretty competent in military drills after five years at VMI."

Dick looked out the window at his older daughters, "What does this mean for our families?"

Jim took a moment and said, "Our wives are strong and have each other. They remember World War I."

Jim stood up and shook Dick's hand in confirmation of their agreement to volunteer for service, and they walked to the door. Jim shouted, "Children, it's time for dinner!" The youngsters were hungry after running around outside.

Everyone sat at the table with one-year-olds Ann and Penny in high chairs. Curly blond, blue eyed Ann was known as Pie Pooh, while dark haired Penny was nicknamed One Cent. Dick carved the pot roast and served it with potatoes and carrots. Green beans, Waldorf salad, and rolls were passed around. The children jabbered away, recapping the afternoon's activities.

After dinner, the Greene family bundled up, said their good-byes and headed home. The boys were spent after a fun day. Although Ann and Jim always enjoyed visits with the Marshalls, they couldn't get the war out of their thoughts.

After a short drive home, the boys helped unload the car. Ann took baby Ann into the house and readied her for bed. The boys brought in some wood. Jimmy went up to take a shower while Billy helped his father lay a fire. "Billy, how did you like the parade?"

"It was cool. I want to be in a parade, not just watching from the side."

"There should be an opportunity for you to march in a parade one day. Do you know why there was a parade today?"

"An important person is in town."

"Do you know who he is and why he is here?"

"Mom said he is Mr. Churchill from England. He is like our president. I don't know why he is here."

"He came to talk to President Roosevelt and Congress about the war. Since the attack in Hawaii, they are discussing plans for the United States to get more involved. Now, the U.S. will send soldiers to help our allies in addition to supplies."

As Jimmy came downstairs, Jim told Billy, "It's your turn to get ready for bed. I'll tell you a story when you are finished." Billy ran upstairs in anticipation of hearing one of his father's stories.

"Jimmy, come enjoy this fire with me."

"Dad, how is the war going to affect us?"

"Son, I'm not sure at the moment but we will have to do our part."

"Will you go away?"

"I don't know. I'm pretty old but I will offer my services. We'll just have to wait and see. Did you have fun today?"

"Yes, my team won!"

When Billy returned, Jim asked, "OK, boys, are you ready for a story?"

"Yes sir."

Jim began, "Daddy Bear, Pooh Bear and their cubs live in the woods near the football field at the Virginia Military Institute in Lexington, Virginia. Today is the biggest football game of the season against Virginia Polytechnic Institute. Lots of people are arriving for the game and setting out their picnics for a tailgate party.

"The Bear Family likes to have company. They have fun watching the cheering and listening to the band play. Their favorite song is The Spirit of VMI."

> Oh, clear the way, VMI is out today,
> We're here to win this game;
> Our team will bring us fame,
> In Alma Mater's name
> For though the odds be against us, we'll not care,
> You'll see us fight the same;
> Always the same old spirit and we'll triumph once again.
> And though defeat seems certain, it's the same with VMI;
> Our battle cry is "Never Never Die."
>
> For when our line starts to weaken, our backs fail to gain,
> Our ends are so crippled, to win seems in vain.
> Then the corps roots the loudest; we'll yet win today.
> The team it will rally and "Fight," Fight," "Fight," "Rau."
> We'll gain through the lines and we'll circle the ends,
> Old Red, White and Yellow will triumph again;
> The "Keydets" will fight 'em and never say die.
> That's the Spirit of VMI.

Daddy continued, "It's the fourth quarter with 30 seconds left and the score is tied. VMI has the ball. The perfect field goal kick is so strong that the football sails over the goal post and lands in the woods. The bear cubs lumber over to get it. There is so much excitement in the stands, nobody sees the bears. They push the ball further into the woods and examine their souvenir. The cubs tumble around and play their version of football, which is more like keep away.

"The triumphant VMI crowd heads toward their cars. When the last vehicle pulls out, the bears head to the trash cans for their dinner and celebrate the big win! The bear cubs keep their prized souvenir for future play."

Jim got up to stoke the fire, "Boys, time to go up."

Billy asked, "Do you think we can go to a basketball game at VMI this year?"

Jim said, "I'll talk to your mother about it. Good night, boys."

"Good night, Daddy."

After the children were tucked in their beds, Ann joined Jim in the living room. He asked his wife, "Ann, did your father enjoy the parade?"

Ann responded, "He thought the bands sounded wonderful! Of course, he is very concerned about what comes next."

Jim said, "I think I should go down to the recruitment office and see what I might do to help. I'm not young at 42, but I may be able to contribute in some way."

Ann picked up her knitting to calm herself, "What if they send you away? Do you expect me to raise three children by myself? How will I do it? Who will tell them stories, throw the baseball, and referee basketball between the boys?"

Jim was thinking out loud while he added a log to the fire, "Maybe I can help train troops nearby and come home on the weekends. The boys will be so busy with school and sports and friends. They're old enough to understand that this war is important and that I need to go."

Ann countered, "But Pie Pooh isn't a year old yet? She requires so much attention and I'm not very young myself at 43."

Jim tried to ease Ann's concerns, "The boys can do a lot for themselves. They are so good with their baby sister, especially Billy. I'll talk to them. We have family and friends to help."

Ann continued with her apprehension "What about the business? Who will take care of the clients? How will we live without your paycheck?"

Jim did his best to alleviate her anxiety. "I can arrange to get a reduced salary from the office and will receive a little military pay. We will make it like everybody else. Where there is a will there is a way." Ann was not convinced she would have enough money to run a household. Her trepidation tempered Jim's optimism. The couple retired for the evening with heavy hearts.

The next day Jim began investigating his options. He talked to several relatives and friends. Most of his male relatives and friends were pondering the inevitable. The war would affect every aspect of life. The complexion of families changed; some went off to war and others entered the work force to fill those vacancies, leaving children without regular caregivers. The economic impact was felt by most, and devasted many families.

Jim discussed his options with his business partner in their advertising agency. Both men had worked judiciously for 15 years to develop a thriving business, with Jim as the main salesperson. They decided to keep the business running. Jim would take a much-reduced salary, until it was unsustainable. After making these arrangements, he went to the recruitment office to sign up.

Once he passed the physical requirements and knew he would be enlisted, he made plans to visit his clients in Pittsburgh, Philadelphia, Baltimore, New York, and a few other cities along the way. He wanted to talk face-to-face to these long-standing business friends to assure them that they would be taken care of while he was away.

Next, Jim focused on the home front. Jim made sure the car was in good running condition, the furnace was working properly, and made necessary repairs around the house. He even added a little fertilizer to his roses.

Ann and Jim spent a long night discussing their finances and creating a budget. There would be less money coming in and additional expenses. Jim reminded Ann that her economical meal planning and sewing skills will be so important to staying within their budget. He made arrangements to purchase a small amount of life insurance, just in case.

Knowing that he might be gone for a while and that they would miss their outings together, Jim made plans to take the boys to a VMI basketball game. After the Saturday chores were complete, Jim said, "Jimmy and Billy, I have a surprise for you."

Billy excitedly responded, "What? What?"

"How about a trip to Lexington?"

Jimmy chimed in, "To see a basketball game?"

Jim responded, "VMI is playing the University of Virginia next Saturday."

Jimmy said, "That should be a good game."

Jim suggested that they invite his best friend, Sam, and his son, Sammy. The boys cheered at that suggestion. Jim said, "Let's walk over and see if they can go with us."

Sam and Jim had grown up together and were in the same class at VMI. Sam went on to Harvard for law school and returned to Washington, D.C. to practice with his father. His son, Sam, was a good friend of the boys.

Martha greeted their friends at the back door, "Hi Jim, Jimmy and Billy. Come on in. Sam and Sammy are in the basement."

Sam heard the conversation and came upstairs. The boys headed downstairs. Sam greeted Jim with a slap on the back. "What brings you over?"

Jim asked, "Would you like to take the boys to VMI to see the basketball game next Saturday?"

Sam looked at Martha, "What do you think?"

Martha checked the calendar, "We don't have any plans. I think that is a grand idea."

Sam turned to Jim, "The trip is approved. What time do you want to leave?"

"Let's get an early start so we can eat lunch and walk around before the game. Ann is going to make a picnic. I'll pick you and Sammy up at 8:00 a.m."

The following Saturday came and their excursion began. It was a four-hour drive through beautiful country to Lexington. With all the leaves off the trees, one could see for miles. The boys kept their eyes peeled for wildlife along the way while Jim and Sam discussed the issues of the day, particularly the effects of the war.

Though VMI was overflowing with students for the 1941-1942 academic year, 90 percent of them were serving in the armed forces by the end of the 1942-43 session. During the war, VMI was used as a training facility for the Army Service Training Program and the Enlisted Reserve Corps. Until 1945, sports and other non-essential activities at VMI were curtailed, so seeing a basketball game during the 1942 season was especially memorable.

Jim and Sam were privy to much war knowledge by virtue of the fact that they were living in Washington, D.C. and had many military contacts, particularly their friend and fellow alumnus, George C. Marshall, the Army's chief of staff. General Marshall organized the largest military expansion in U.S. history. He became secretary of state after the war and later received the Nobel Peace Prize in 1953 for advocating a significant U.S. economic and political commitment to post-war European recovery, known as the Marshall plan.

The carload bound for VMI arrived in Lexington at noon with ravenous appetites. They found a warm location on campus to eat their lunch. Ann made fried chicken and deviled eggs while Martha sent ham biscuits and chocolate chip cookies. The boys and their fathers made short work of the picnic.

After lunch, the group walked over to the equestrian riding hall which was under construction. They stopped to give a few apples and sugar cubes to the horses. Jim and Sam shared childhood stories of horseback riding at Spring Hill Farm, where Sam had been a frequent visitor.

During those summer vacations, on many days, young Jim and Sam and the dog made a trip to the train station. They took along a cart to pick up any mail or packages on the two-mile trip. When they got older, the boys rode horses and used saddlebags to carry the parcels. They spent hours riding through the woods, stopping to eat their sack lunch and fishing in the creek. Jim loved looking for animals, particularly bears. They spent many nights in a small canvas tent, listening to the wildlife.

The game was starting soon, so the men and boys left the horses and practiced marching to the gym. Since the UVA and VMI teams were from schools only an hour apart and many fans lived nearby, the place was packed. The VMI band was building enthusiasm with its pre-game music. Everyone was excited due to this long running rivalry. The game was well worth the long trip, as VMI narrowly won in the last few minutes.

The gang headed for an early dinner at their favorite local restaurant, the Southern Inn. They feasted on vegetable beef soup, homemade rolls, and hot fudge sundaes. After their hearty meal and a full day of fun and excitement, the boys were asleep before Jim left the Blue Ridge Mountains in Rockbridge County.

During the drive home, Jim and Sam recapped the game and the changes at VMI. When they were certain the boys were asleep, they talked of their immediate futures. Sam and Jim knew they would support the war in some capacity. Sam planned to participate in Judge Advocate General's Corps. Jim thought he might help organize and train troops.

Another Saturday found the Greene boys at one of their favorite places: the National Zoo, located in Rock Creek Park. The 163-acre site is one of the oldest zoos in the country, founded in 1889. Jimmy and Billy wandered through the zoo with their father and talked about the animals. When Jim wasn't telling his own stories about animals, he read books about them to the boys. One of their favorites was Rudyard Kipling's "The Jungle Book," and the trips to the zoo gave the boys a real sense of the size of the elephants, giraffes and tigers. They could almost picture Mogli's adventures. They especially liked the bears, who stole their hearts because of their father's bear stories and cartoons.

While the boys were out for the afternoon, Ann invited a few friends over for lunch and bridge while baby Ann napped. Along with Jim, their husbands would serve in the armed forces during the war. The four friends supported each other throughout the war. Florence was Jim's cousin. She and her husband had three daughters. Dick Marshall, cousin of General Marshall and an attorney, served in the Pacific Theatre. Martha and Sam Syme had one son. He served as an attorney on General Patton's staff. Another of Jim's cousins, Elizabeth Beale Leahy, and her husband had two children. William "Bill" Leahy served in the Navy with his father. Admiral William Daniel Leahy, the senior most military officer on active duty during World War II. He was at the center of all major military decisions during the war.

An April Easter Saturday found the Greene family at the annual Beale Easter Egg hunt at Oak Hill Cemetery in Georgetown. Oak Hill, the final resting place of many ancestors, was located near the family homes in Georgetown. The Easter Egg Hunt was a long-standing tradition. The massive ancient creviced trees and the old tombstones were great hiding places for colored eggs, and the Beale cousins spent the afternoon in spirited play in a park-like setting.

Sundays found the Greene family alternating visits between Jim's relatives and Ann's family, where they spent Easter this year. After Ann's father's retirement, her parents moved from their home in Danville, Virginia, to Washington, D.C. to live with one of their three daughters, Mary Baber, and her husband. They lived in a spacious apartment in the Ontario, a Beaux Arts landmark, located in the Lanier Heights neighborhood.

One Sunday, Jimmy and Billy raced to the front door of the apartment to see who could ring the doorbell first. Grandfather Edgar answered the door to two out of breath boys. "Hi Granddaddy!" After hugs were shared and they waited for the rest of the family, Granddaddy asked, "What card game shall we play today?"

"I want to play poker and win lots of money!" shouted Billy.

"Shhh, you'll bother the neighbors. We'll play poker. Maybe Julian has some Brazilian currency for you. He just returned from Sao Paolo." Mary's husband, Julian, worked for the Treasury Department and his job took him to many foreign countries. The boys loved to hear stories of his travels and adventures. At the time he was investigating counterfeit currency which was a critical issue because Germany was forging money to finance German intelligence operations. The counterfeit money was laundered in exchange for real currency and other assets.

Aunt Mary walked out of the kitchen, wiped her hands on a dishtowel, and welcomed everybody. Jimmy asked, "What's for dessert?"

Aunt Mary answered, "What does it smell like?"

Jimmy guessed, "Pie?"

Aunt Mary prodded, "What kind?"

Jimmy replied, "Pecan?"

Aunt Mary congratulated him, "Jimmy, you have a bloodhound's nose."

Billy remarked, "My favorite!"

Aunt Mary voiced her expectation, "I know you will eat all of your dinner so you can have a piece!"

Ann and Jim followed Edgar into the living room to find Grandmother sitting at a jigsaw puzzle. Jimmy sat down to help while the adults continued their own conversations.

After a fun afternoon of games, the Greene family packed up for the drive home and said their good-byes. Jim and Edgar shook hands and shared a look of concern. Jim promised, "I will stay in touch to the best of my ability. You will be an important support for Ann."

A month later, Jim got the call to report for active duty. He had one week before his departure.

Jim sat down with his sons. "Jimmy and Billy, I need to talk to you about something very serious. Since Pearl Harbor was attacked, the United States has been ramping up its commitment in the war. I have been called to serve."

Jimmy chimed in, "Dad, when are you leaving and how long will you be gone? Who will help Mom around the house and tend the roses?"

Jim responded, "Son, I am leaving next week. I will be gone at least six months. I will be gone as long as I can help. It depends how quickly we can win this war. You and Billy will have to help Mother with your sister and with the chores around the house."

Billy hung his head, "Who will coach me in baseball? Who will help me work on my basketball shot? Who will tell me adventure stories?"

"Billy, your rec coach will help you with baseball and basketball. Remember, you know the basics. Practice will make you better. I will write about my adventures."

Jim gave his sons a big hug. He closed with a cheerful, "Now, let's enjoy our time before I leave!"

Jim made one more important visit. He went to the old family home in Georgetown to see his stepfather, Walter, who had married his mother when Jim was seven years old. Walter loved Jim and his brother, Albert, as if they were his biological children. Jim and Walter stayed in close contact after his mother, Ellen, died in 1932. About once a week, Jim met Walter and his half-brother, Walter, for a beer at Clyde's, one of their favorite neighborhood spots.

Jim walked pensively up the long staircase to the door of his old Georgetown home. He entered the house to find a bespectacled Walter at his desk, looking over architectural drawings. He rose to shake Jim's hand. "Welcome Jim. Let's go out to the garden and enjoy the cherry blossoms. It's time for me to put this project to rest for today."

Jim recalled fond memories from his childhood and during the period following college graduation. He lived with his mother and Walter for several years while getting his business started. "Walter, I remember many fun parties with our family and neighbors in this house. Thank you for allowing me to live here after college. Looking back, it really helped me get the business going."

Walter asked, "What are they going to do without you?"

Jim answered, "I've visited as many clients as possible. They'll make do. Hopefully, I won't be gone too long."

Walter continued, "What are your plans?"

Jim responded, "I think I am headed to North Carolina to help get the troops ready for deployment. I leave on Saturday."

Walter said, "Together the United States and Britain will win this war with the combined leadership both countries have. I know the troops you train will be ready with your VMI background."

Jim thanked Walter for his confidence and support. They said their good-byes, and Jim went home to his family.

Jim's day of departure was a warm spring day with budding trees and blooming flowers. Ann snapped a picture before they left for Union Station. The boys were dressed in their Saturday play clothes. Jimmy, with an unhappy demeanor, wore a short-sleeved white knit shirt, jeans and tennis shoes. Billy, with a sad downcast face, had on a blue and white striped t-shirt, shorts and tennis shoes. Baby Ann was in a hand-made smocked dress, with her white learning-how-to-walk shoes. Jim, standing erect with a serious expression and slight smile, was dressed in a khaki shirt and tie, a dark green military uniform and black dress shoes. His garrison cap and appropriate dress pins finished his ensemble.

Jim put his duffle bag in the trunk. The boys climbed in the back seat. Ann with the baby on her lap sat in the front. Jim started the car for the ten-mile drive to the train station. On the way, Jim led them in singing the VMI song.

The parking lot at Union Station was full of families dropping off their fathers, brothers and sons. Many parents, girlfriends, wives, and children were milling around the terminal. The Greene family made its way to the platform. Jim's last words before he boarded the train, "Keep your chins up and help each other. I will write often." He found a window seat and gave a final salute as the train pulled out. The boys returned the salute while Ann joined them in waving and yelling good-bye.

Jim was not the only one of the family whose life changed dramatically during the war.

Ann and the children also found themselves in a very different environment. Washington, D.C. became the major hub of wartime workers spread all around the city. Soon after Pearl Harbor, construction of the Pentagon was accelerated in order to combine the war department and the miliary leadership offices. Thousands of architects, engineers, draftsmen and construction workers completed the enormous complex in 16 months.

Women from across the country came to replace men and fill new stateside military and government positions. City officials scrambled to build temporary housing. Many homeowners rented rooms to these new arrivals.

Blackouts were mandatory due to a bombing threat on the nation's capital. The Capitol and other buildings were darkened. Cut-off switches were installed on streetlights in case of air attacks. Homeowners were required to darken their homes at night. Older city residents were trained and acted as an auxiliary police force and stationed throughout neighborhoods to make sure residents were complying. Sirens were a constant reminder of the war and a potential attack on the city. Along with their fellow Washingtonians, the Greenes settled into a very different lifestyle – one that lasted until the war ended in 1945.

Chapter 4
Attention!

Once in North Carolina, Captain Greene learned that he was going west to Texas. He spent a week traveling with fellow soldiers on a train through Birmingham, Alabama; New Orleans, Louisiana; and Dallas, Texas. Jim gathered a wealth of information from many conversations and experiences during the trip. He spent hours listening to soldiers recount their personal stories. Delays due to troop movements and an unintended detour around Birmingham extended the journey by 1,800 miles and gave Jim ample time to get to know and build comradery with other soldiers headed to Texas.

Jim's fellow passengers had many tales of their war experiences. For example, Lieutenant Mike Smiley, headed home with a gunshot wound to the leg, shared his story of the Pacific Theater. Smiley's sense of gratitude was evident: "I am one of the lucky ones." He had fought in the Battle of the Java Sea, where many of his fellow sailors lost their lives. It was a decisive naval battle, where Allied navies suffered a disastrous defeat at the hand of the Imperial Japanese Navy on February 27, 1942. This and other Allied losses led to Japanese occupation of the entire Dutch East Indies.

Lieutenant John McChord compared his experience at Java Sea with his service as Leahy's orderly during the battle of Brest, France, in World War I. Brest served as the American Naval Headquarters in France. Major achievements took place at this location. John commiserated, "Being on the winning side is so much easier for the morale."

Taking a long-range perspective, Jim responded, "Leahy is a patient man with a steady hand. Battles will be lost. We have to persevere and stay strong in the fight." Then to lighten the mood he suggested, "Let's go to dinner." The two returning service men joined Jim and his seatmate, Lieutenant Jack

Hillsman, as they made their way to the dining car. After their evening meal, a card game was their nightly entertainment.

As the train made its way through Alabama, Jim recalled the stories of his Grandmother Fanny's train ride from Alabama to Washington, D.C. during the Civil War. Fanny's mother died in childbirth and her father died when she was only two years old. Her maternal grandmother raised her until the grandmother's death. At the age of 14, Fanny went to live with her father's family in Washington, D.C. Jim imagined what it must have been like for a young girl to be drawn away from the life she knew in Alabama and sent to live with a new set of relatives in an unfamiliar city. Fanny showed the fearlessness and courage Jim knew he would need for his wartime service.

Jim was shaken from his thoughts by the jolt of the train coming to a stop in New Orleans. The men were relieved to have three hours in the city. It gave them just enough time to arrange to share a hotel room where they could take showers. A nap would have been nice but there was no rest for the weary travelers. Unbeknownst to Jim, these small inconveniences would not compare to what lay ahead.

The last leg of the train journey was in front of them, beginning with crossing the mouth of the Mississippi River on a rickety bridge that was a mile long. Jim wrote to Ann, "We crossed Ol' Man River and the train began to shake."

Besides descriptions of his travel experiences, financial concerns were a recurring theme in the letters between Jim and Ann. He was responsible for his travel expenses and then would be reimbursed. Jim's last correspondence while traveling to Texas began with this continuing worry about monetary matters, "My money is almost gone as they only gave us tickets to North Carolina. I will collect five cents a mile as soon as I catch a finance officer. I had to cash a check for $15.00." This was not a trivial amount. In 1942, $15 would be equivalent to $237 today.

Jim, Jack Hillsman, and five other men were all going to Sheppard Field, located five miles north of Wichita Falls, Texas, and ten miles from the Oklahoma border. This flat area experienced long, hot summers with temperatures regularly over 100 degrees. Sheppard Field had some of the highest summer daily maximum temperatures in the entire U.S., outside the southwest deserts.

The conditions at Sheppard Field inspired the following poem by an unknown cadet.

The Ode of Sheppard Field

Out on the windswept desert,
Old Sheppard's the spot,
Battling the terrible dust storms
In the land that God forgot.

Down in the brush with our rifles,
Down in the ditch with our picks,
Doing the work of inmates
And too damn exhausted to kick.

Out with the cowboys,
Out where the boys get blue,
Out on the windswept desert,
A thousand miles from you!

At night the wind keeps blowing,
It's more than we can stand,
No! We are not convicts,
We're defenders of our land.

We are "CADETS" of the Air Corps,
Earning our meager pay,
Guarding people with millions,
For seventy cents a day.

No one knows we're living,
No one gives a damn,
Back home it's soon forgotten,
We're but loaned to Uncle Sam.

We're living for tomorrow,
Only to see our gals,
Hoping when we get to them,
They are not married to our pals.

Only three years can we stand it,
Three years of life we'll miss,
Boy! Don't let the draft board get you,
And for God's sake don't enlist.

A continuously rotating population of 35,000 men occupied the base. Jim and his fellow officers recognized their mission. "We are the first unit of over-age combat officers assigned to the camp. We think our gang is going to start a training system to make soldiers out of grease monkeys and mechanics."

Due to a measles epidemic among the soldiers, Jim could not live on base. He and Lieutenant Archie, a professor at Wake Forest University, found a room with the Rundell family in Wichita Falls. The men took over their second bedroom, vacated by the Rundells' son, who was about to receive his pilot's wings. Eventually five officers would fill the house. All shared one bathroom. Getting around was also a challenge. Since Jim didn't have a car, he was dependent on public transportation or found rides when the bus wasn't running.

Meanwhile, Ann's letters kept Jim abreast of life at home, "I'm missing you dreadfully and nothing breaks the loneliness. The family is bringing supper to keep me from being lonely. It's been the longest week I ever spent."

The children's lives continued with some small accomplishments. "Pie Pooh climbed the stairs today and says, 'Daddy gone bye-bye.' Billy is helping Jim with his paper route. They are ready for the school year to end. The porch project is almost finished and will give me a nice place to sit this summer. Your roses are lovely. Do keep well and write as often as you can."

Ann and Jim were conscious of every expenditure and every small economy. They stayed in touch without paying for postage stamps as letters to or from service personnel were delivered free of charge. Their limited budget made purchasing necessities difficult. A few stores gave out credit cards to build loyalty but were very strict during wartime, not allowing unpaid charges to extend longer than 30 days. Some shops would give military discounts. Jim sent Ann cards for use at the Post Exchange at home.

Ann had the oil changed and the tank filled with gas before gasoline rationing began in May of 1942, as she was only allocated three gallons per week. After that, a car owner had to certify to a local board that gas was a necessity and that he or she owned no more than five tires in order to qualify for ration stamps. A sticker was then affixed to the windshield designating the vehicle's allowance.

Back in Texas, Jim was assigned to work for Colonel John Clements in the Replacement Center. He was the Plans and Training Officer for the 405th Special Technical School Squadron. The squadron was comprised of 1,000 to 1,600 men divided into five flights, with a turnover of 300 new men each week.

One of Jim's responsibilities was helping train the officers in infantry. Upon completion, these officers left to start 12 new training centers in different parts of the United States. The five-week training consisted of basic military general orders and conduct indoctrination, familiarization with all standard weapons, rifle range qualification, and physical training with obstacle courses and gas masks.

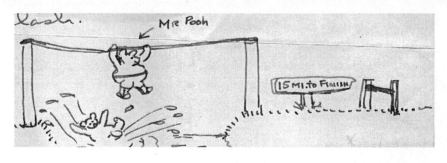

Jim shared his thoughts on the difficulties of training in a note to a former VMI classmate, Lieutenant Colonel Doug Johnson, "The advanced flight is just smart enough to try and dodge work, while the new flight is being taught how to take a shower. The strange thing is I was all worried about the war before I got in, now days go by without me realizing one is going on."

Jim's days began at 6:00 a.m., with every fourth day beginning at 5:00 a.m. They ended at 6:30 p.m. He only worked half a day on Sunday. He was the only drill sergeant and his routine was to carry on infantry drill three hours in the morning and two hours in the afternoon in unrelenting heat and blowing sand. "We just eat another salt tablet and keep 'em flying. We are working the soldiers very hard to make them tough and able to fight soon. Everybody is anxious to go someplace like Germany or Japan to get at the people who started it." Jim spent his other hours in classes or on administrative tasks.

After paying him a compliment for his work, the colonel gave Jim his first big assignment. "Jim, thank you for helping prepare for General Walter Weaver's visit and inspection. He was satisfied with our progress in getting this operation underway. Would you please organize a parade in Wichita Falls for Flag Day?" Flag Day is celebrated on June 14th to commemorate the adoption of the flag of the United States on June 14, 1777 by resolution of the

Second Continental Congress. The U.S. Army celebrates its birthday on this day, too.

"Yes sir."

Jim took the 405th and 410th rifles to Wichita Falls for the parade. Red Cross nurses, the American Legion, fire engines, and the local high school band followed the Army.

Jimmy and Billy remembered Jim with notes and gifts on Father's Day. They reported that they kept up their grades at school and were helping around the house, taking over chores as best they could. Billy watched over his baby sister while Jimmy helped with meals.

Jim spent Father's Day gearing up for the next phase of activity. "The game seems to be: catch the next man with his pants down. Night orders demanded 50 rifles from the advanced flight for the next day's parade. The advanced flight had no rifle training. We only had a few hours to train. I figured I had about a week to train another group. The next night a 'Red Ball' order came sending 300 men to a P.O.E. (Port of Embarkation), including all of my trained riflemen. Another madhouse ensued." 'Red Ball' referred to a critical need for manpower and P.O.E. was a location in which soldiers were sent abroad. Another afternoon on the drill field Jim was interrupted by Captain Cavit: "Have three flights trained for a mass review of ten squadrons in an hour."

"Yes sir."

Jim was drilling 144 men with strict orders not to leave the field. He needed 288 more men. He sent runners to retrieve men from lectures, from the firing range, and from the infirmary where they were getting vaccinations. Three flights were ready by the skin of his teeth. The stakes were high. If one didn't meet the command, he could be threatened or punished.

One of Jim's roles was serving as "Officer on Duty" for 24 hours every fourth day. He used a bicycle to inspect the post as he didn't have a car. His responsibilities included guard details, prisoner counts, shake down inspections, night post inspections of sentinels ready to shoot, and guarding millions of dollars' worth of equipment. While he was on duty one night, the PX was robbed. The robber was caught and Jim had to participate in another court.

After six weeks in Texas, Jim took over the squadron of two captains, six lieutenants, and three flights. One of his first tasks was managing payday. He paid the men in cash, giving them money to buy alcohol, which led to argumentative behavior. After a few days all hell broke loose. Under the 104th article of war, he had maximum punishment authority, short of throwing a man in the stockade.

One of the crises involved a couple of boys who decided to kill each other with knives and caused quite an uproar. Jim threatened them with hanging, and it scared them sober. He put a guard over them and shipped them off to war in the morning, instead of having them sent to the stockade.

He shared his sense of accountability with Ann.

"I know so little and I am having so much thrown at me that any spare moment is spent learning. The responsibility piles up and a good soldier never fails. When the boys leave; they don't know where they are going. I can guess based on the desert equipment or Arctic stuff that they are loading on the train. They study and fight for jobs that carry a 50% chance of coming home, so I know my training has to click.

"Thank the boys for their nice letters and give the little Pie Pooh a big hug and a kiss. As for the Mamu Bear, you are the sweetest and loveliest creature in the world. I love you more and more the longer I stay away. I hope you don't get mad at your very negligent and sassy, fat husband who runs off to lovely and exciting adventures and leaves you with all the drudgery and worry. I'm feeling like an irresponsible puppy dog instead of a dutiful daddy bear."

While taking on more duties as head of the squadron, Jim had more contact with Colonel Clements, who was making quite a reputation for himself. The Replacement Center was known as the Clements Concentration Camp by men assigned to other areas of Sheppard Field. The Colonel's slogan, tacked up around the camp, was "The difficult will be done immediately; the impossible takes a little longer."

Jim dealt with many personnel issues with little time to analyze before making major decisions. For example, he had ten minutes to interview six men and certify their ability and unquestionable loyalty. He approved or disapproved furloughs for death, marriage, financial and business matters as fast as he could scan the requests. He judged men as truthful or liars based on facial expressions and would mete out punishment not really knowing for sure how just or unjust, he had been.

After eight weeks, Jim was elevated to commanding officer of the 407th Squadron with two captains, two lieutenants, and 1,200 men under him. "The fat daddy, who wanted to play with soldiers, hit the jackpot. I DIDN'T KNOW THERE COULD BE SO MANY ROOKIES!"

His first major challenge as commanding officer was the arrival of an additional 800 flying cadets. The cadets got stuck waiting for vacancies at flying fields or a mix-up in their records. According to Jim, the pilots were arrogant and thought they were superior to the infantrymen, looking on them as earthworms. As a result, they were pulled out of other squadrons where their attitudes were distracting and a bad influence. Jim's assignment was to address this unacceptable behavior. They had to learn to work together for the safety of all; in war when life was on the line, rank made no difference.

Life at the base was not all work and training. Jim took time to help build camaraderie by organizing a softball team to give the boys a break from their routine. The squadron team won the camp championship with 17 consecutive victories. A gala celebration took place in a nearby hotel. It did seem a bit strange, and not as celebratory without women.

Ann adjusted to a new routine at home. The family Fourth of July party was held at the Greenes' house. The Beale cousins were excited about getting together again. They dressed in red, white, and blue with paper hats made by the girls for the parade. The four older boys, Jimmy and Billy Greene, Bobby Leahy, and Johnny Bennett attached playing cards to the spokes of their bikes to make noise. Louise Leahy, the oldest cousin, pulled the three youngest, Ann Greene, Penny Marshall, and Robert Bennett, in a red wagon. The other two girls, Mary Mallory and Sophie Marshall, shook brightly colored rattles as they danced along the route. Their mothers led them in singing patriotic songs. The neighbors, flying their American flags, came out of their houses and joined in celebration.

After the parade, Ann served an early picnic dinner outside. The three Beale sisters, Elizabeth Leahy, Sophie Bennett and Florence Marshall contributed to the meal. The smell of fried chicken and other goodies mingled with the lingering scent of roses. The only male in the family still in town, Louise and Billy Leahy's grandfather, Admiral Leahy, set off a few fireworks for the children.

Ann sent Jim a few requested items, including his service record, pajamas, and a few pictures from the Fourth of July celebration. She was worried about Admiral Leahy, who did not look well. "I'm afraid he's going to have to die for his country as much as any soldier who gets shot. It's a shame for a man who has given such splendid service and earned a well-deserved rest." After losing his wife in Vichy, France, where Admiral Leahy had been serving as

U.S. Ambassador, he was called back to active duty at the age of 70 to serve as the highest ranking active member of the U.S. military from 1942 until 1949.

"Things are routine and nothing has fallen on my head yet," Jim wrote Ann. He got through his first court martial as accusing officer, without a hitch. A court martial is a military judicial body for trying a member of the armed services accused of an offense against military law. Jim would preside over many courts-martial in the years to come.

There were always cultural adjustments for a man from the east coast. Jim felt that the tall and lean Texas and Oklahoma boys with lifeguard tans would be very capable with a little training, and his experience proved that to be the case. Occasionally, a sergeant complained about making a compulsory allotment to his wife: "He couldn't see why a woman would need money."

Drinking was another issue as illustrated by Jim's comment in another letter: "One of my sergeants spends all his money on liquor. He passes out every night but is right on beam at 5:00 a.m. so we get along fine."

After working for almost three months, Jim enjoyed his second full day off. He spent the day on the Rundells' porch enjoying a cool afternoon, reading and catching up on correspondence with family and friends. He encouraged Ann to write a thank you note to Mrs. Rundell for being so nice to her house guests.

At the end of August, Ann and Jim celebrated their 12th anniversary with their first phone call since his enlistment. They commiserated over the first combat fatality within their circle of friends and neighbors. "We must be more grimly determined to wind this one up properly – no matter how long, no matter what cost."

Unfortunately, the boys weren't home to talk over the phone with their father. Jim closed with, "If I were a lady bear, I would bellow and bawl. I feel so far away from the den. I love you so much it hurts so stay waiting at the k-k-kitchen door. It won't be too long."

As the war geared up, Jim suggested that Ann purchase necessities, as much as possible, for the coming year. "Future shortages will make everything expensive, if obtainable at all. Civilian supplies will bog down completely and probably won't pick up until quite a time after the war is won."

Jim learned that the stipend from the business would end immediately as it was unsustainable. He advised Ann that she "keep three or four hundred dollars in case of emergency and if there is any money left, buy government bonds.

The money situation will be bad when it's only captain's pay and no money from the office. It's very little to live on in two places. The new taxes will throw our nest egg into an omelet. I'm betting we will still eat, which is all that matters."

Jim was learning lessons about leadership. He found out what the cost was for giving a break to a few men. The first involved an AWOL (absent without leave) attempt. A soldier bought another soldier's pass, dyed his hair, and tried to escape through the sewer grate. After he was caught, Jim made arrangements to ship him out, instead of slapping him with charges.

Discussion with the commanding officer resulted in approval of another shipping order. This other situation made Jim a horrible example for failing to give enough punishment. Colonel Clements reprimanded Jim at an officer's meeting for this decision. A private got a hotel room in town to get drunk. He ran out of liquor and accidentally put on a sergeant's shirt to go get more liquor. He was caught by the military police and charged with public drunkenness in another's uniform. Jim didn't give him a court-martial but a lesser punishment. "There are many ways to catch hell even when you do your best," he wrote.

After living for five months in the Rundell home, Jim was able to move on base in mid-October. He was thrilled to live in a small building with two bedrooms and a bathroom. The officers' mess hall and club were next door. He relished getting a little more sleep in his own room.

The move to the base also gave Jim time to prepare for his next assignment: Miami. He shared his perspective at this juncture with Ann.

"I will do whatever is needed wherever I am sent. If the best men go, there will be less widows and orphans. Ability is far more important in war than friendship. We are all numbers and have to fit into sequence. We need to win the war so we will have families. If we don't win, history won't be written in English.

"I'm thinking about Christmas presents. I thought about buying cowboy boots for the boys and a pair of little white ones for Pie Pooh. It seems foolish at times like these. Real shoes and bacon are needed and a captain's pay looks smaller and smaller. Don't get wrinkles worrying.

"The next time you write I will be at a new station. I can't tell you when I'm leaving or arriving. Don't be surprised if a big check comes through our bank account. We pay our own way and are reimbursed later."

And then a great surprise arrived in a telegram for Ann: November 20, 1942

ARRIVE WASHINGTON, D.C. SUNDAY NIGHT 3 DAY STOPOVER

Chapter 5
Lessons to Learn

After a three-day train trip from Texas, Jim arrived in Washington, D.C. to celebrate the Thanksgiving holiday with his family. Suntanned Jim shared his experiences with the boys while he threw the football in the yard and shot baskets in the driveway. He played horsey with little Ann. Jim took the time to visit with other family members. He had a drink with his cousins, Florence Marshall and Liz Leahy, and told them about his next assignment. He learned that Dick Marshall and Billy Leahy were heading to the Pacific Theatre. He visited his stepfather, Walter, who was slowing down at 74, but still had his keen mind.

After a whirlwind three-day visit and early Thanksgiving lunch with Ann's family, the Greenes headed to the train station once again. This departure caused more anxiety for Ann as she didn't know what the future held. Jimmy and Billy were so happy to spend time with their father that saying good-bye again was traumatic. They knew the stakes were higher as their father could go overseas for an indefinite period of time and be posted to a place much more dangerous than Texas.

The sad departure, the long train trip to Miami, and thoughts of Officer Candidate School, found Jim thinking about his VMI days. His college application acknowledged his challenge with academics. His five-year struggle to graduate made him anxious about returning to school and grades. He knew that he had much to learn to serve in another capacity. School was necessary in order to have the knowledge to make the best contribution.

Jim arrived in Miami to a warm welcome. A crowd from Sheppard Field made him feel like he was almost returning to a VMI reunion in a South Sea setting. He described the Florida environment. "This place is more beautiful than I ever imagined. One of our drill fields is a golf course. I've been in the surf twice and I am full of seafood. Jimmy and Billy would love to climb the coconut trees."

The reunion quickly began to resemble a school term. Jim paid $300 in rent for a six-week stay. He lived with Lt. Snowden and Lt. Brookfield in a small room with windows tightly covered due to blackout regulations. It didn't take Jim long to be overwhelmed with his studies. He wished for Ann's brains, especially as the twelve-week course was condensed into six weeks.

The academic format was similar to college with classes, homework, and exams. The subjects covered aspects of squadron oversight, such as mess management, disciplinary procedures, and financial issues. One type of combat practice was an air drone strike. The air drone strikes were target practice for bomb drops as accuracy was paramount to saving civilian lives. Jim learned about ammunition, prisoners, traffic, building things, and burying the dead. His six-month assignment at Sheppard Field helped him.

However, Florida without snow, Christmas trees, or people shopping, was quite different from any of Jim's holidays in the past. The tropical weather, 100 soldiers to every civilian, and the blackouts were a significant change from last Christmas. Jim told his children that he would watch out for Santa Claus since he was on guard duty Christmas Eve.

Christmas morning was spent opening a multitude of cards and presents sent from family and friends. He shared his peanuts, candy and cigarettes with his fellow OCS students.

Later in the day, Jim was invited for a boat ride around Biscayne Bay. The large estates with their verdant gardens were exquisite. Unfortunately for those who owned yachts, the Navy took their leisure boats to patrol the waters off the coast.

Jim sent a photograph of himself to his family so that they would know he was with them in spirit. He always drew personal cartoons for each of them and had fond memories of seeing his children's joy when opening presents on Christmas morning. "The little Pie Pooh will have a time with the boys trying to show her everything. I am glad Jim is so thoughtful and Bill is so kindhearted. I know they will have a sweet time."

Ann placed Jim's picture on the mantel to watch over the Bear den. She struggled more than usual with Jim's absence during this Christmas holiday while taking care of their sick children without his help. She missed Jim terribly but found the fortitude to carry on. Ann supported the war effort and trusted that Jim would make good decisions, but the fear of losing him came to the fore as the potential risks were elevated.

At this special family time, Jim was at a point in which he questioned his decision to enlist. He had second thoughts and reservations about the choices that he made. He had gotten himself into a situation that he didn't expect. Being in combat was much different than training troops on US soil. Preparing to potentially go abroad made going to a war zone more of a reality. He was conflicted between being responsible to his family, being patriotic, or just being on an adventure. Overall, in these times of doubt, he felt that he must not waiver in his allegiance to the cause, the country, and the world.

On December 31st, Jim stopped by the Officer's Club to have a New Year's Eve drink at midnight to recreate some sense of previous celebrations. He felt the loss when he remembered the annual family New Year's Eve party. "I felt rather sad about old times when I heard 'Auld Lang Syne.'" Jim missed not being with his relatives and friends as in times past, but he knew many of the men in his family would be serving too.

After successfully completing the OCS academic requirements in the middle of the pack of 500 officers, he had to take an intensive physical fitness exam and scored a 66 out of 100.

The average age of the class was 34 years old, quite a bit younger than Jim. As he wrote to Ann with a hint of pride, "Your skinny little husband was sixteen points better than the average in running, jumping, chinning, etc. In comparison that really makes him practically a 30-year-old in spite of my 43 summers. If I'm not so good in the head, I'm at least in pretty good shape otherwise."

Jim wondered where his next assignment would take him. The Air Corps seemed to send their personnel to a series of schools for training in different aspects of warfare to make sure they were proficient. He considered the possibility of getting closer to home and the opportunity for another visit as he was really missing his family. He learned that all but thirteen of the 100 men in his group would return to their old stations, so he began to think that he would be sent back to Sheppard Field.

January 10, 1943, the day before graduation, Jim learned that he would return to Sheppard Field temporarily. Given short notice, he scurried around to get enough money to purchase a train ticket. The Post exchange would only cash a check for $25 and a train ticket cost more so he got a friend to cash another $25 check.

The train headed out of Florida, passing old trees covered in Spanish moss, hollies and pines. Jim's Pullman car had 29 officers headed for Sheppard Field or Amarillo, Texas. Amarillo was home to the Air Corps Technical School which was established to train Flying Fortress mechanics and technicians. They worked on the Boeing B-17 Flying Fortress, a heavy bomber. Heavy bombers were aircraft capable of delivering the largest payload, usually bombs, and had the longest range of their era. These bombers played a major role in the monumental shift on the war front.

The Allied leadership focused their efforts in the Middle Eastern Theatre. President Roosevelt secretly met with Winston Churchill and others at the Casablanca Conference in Morocco January 14 to 24, 1943, to plan the Allied European strategy for the next phase of World War II. The conference agenda addressed the specifics of tactical procedure, allocation of resources, and the broader issues of diplomatic policy. The debate and negotiations produced what was known as the Casablanca Declaration, and perhaps its most historically provocative statement of purpose, "unconditional surrender." The doctrine of unconditional surrender came to represent the unified voice of implacable Allied will—the determination that the Axis powers would be fought to their ultimate defeat.

Around the same time, Jim received a forwarded letter that his friend, Sam, had written to his son, Jimmy. Sam served on Patton's staff in the Mediterranean Sea. General Patton led the forces at Casablanca during Operation Torch. Operation Torch was the first mass involvement of US troops in the European-North African Theatre and saw the first airborne assault carried out by the United States. Sam had a great vantage point to observe that operation.

"Dear Jimmie,

We had front row seats for an exceedingly interesting battle. When a sixteen-inch shell hit the water about 50 yards from my ship, I decided that I would rather see such battles from a seat in a movie theatre. It isn't fun seeing these devils way up beyond anti-aircraft range and then the little black dot leaves the lane and heads in your direction. You feel pretty darn helpless. When those big naval guns let go, they actually make the ocean tremble. It is quite a sight to see a cruiser let go with its eight or ten-inch guns, and then a big battle wagon off on the horizon lets go with her sixteen-inchers. I actually saw the shells traveling through the air. The big ones catch up and pass the little ones.

We landed early one morning and they were still fighting to beat the band.

When I went over the side of the ship with full field equipment, including a tommy-gun and 100 rounds of ammunition I sure wished I had had a little time on those obstacle courses. I found that I am not too old to hit the ground and hit it in a hurry when the necessity arises. I also found out these doggone tin hats are mighty handy for digging holes when you need a hole in a hurry. When those planes fly low and fast, you crave a nice hole more than anything else in the world, unless it is to be somewhere else. Staff work can be pretty interesting on a staff like this because this bird (Patton) doesn't believe in setting up headquarters way behind the lines. His headquarters is a tank and expects his staff within yelling distance.

Sonny, when I get home, if I ever try to tell you or anyone else, that I was not scared, you just give a loud Bronx cheer. I was scared plenty, but before the day was over, I was managing to have a pretty good time. There is an awful lot that I can't tell you now but I am writing in my little book every day. When I get home, I will be able to give you the works.

We are in an interesting city. It seems strange to see Arabs running around amidst modern architecture. They wear long cloaks with hoods and the usual fez. About half of the people are French and the other half are Arabs. We had a big parade with the combined American and French armies. We are quite friendly now though we shot the deuce out of each other for about four days. The civilian population is swell to us. They are so glad to get rid of the Germans and the Italians that they give us anything we want.

Affectionately,
Sam"

Jim appreciated Sam's thoughtfulness in writing to Jimmy and treasured the letter. He sent it back to Jimmy and told him not to lose it. Jim thought Sam was fortunate to work with General Patton. He acknowledged that Sam was in the thick of things and had plenty of excitement, as well as plenty of danger. He wondered if he would head in that direction and if their paths would cross.

While waiting for his orders, Jim lived in a dormitory room in bachelor officers' quarters at Sheppard Field. The little building that had been his former home was taken over by two married couples. He fantasized that perhaps Ann could join him and they could live in similar quarters. "If I'm still here when the kids finish school, I think it would be best for you to come down here. I couldn't stand it much longer without you…"

The temperature at Sheppard had dropped precipitously from 125 during the last summer. Now in January it hovered in the teens. The water pipes in the officers' quarters were frozen "My kindest regards to Mr. Sheep. I think I'm one jump from a cold storage chicken all day. It really must be quite a relief to be shot while playing around in Russia at 40 degrees below." Jim did not like cold weather and appreciated his warm wool clothing.

But despite the change in the temperature, Jim enjoyed some aspects of life on the base. For a little variety and to talk with the soldiers, Jim went to a mess hall lunch and chowed on a delectable meal of noodle soup, chicken with dressing, peas, bread, cherry pie with ice cream and coffee. He thought the U.S. Army was the best fed army in the world, at least when they were on American soil.

Jim joined in the typical weekly 10-mile road march. The training involved flour sack drops from airplanes, tear gas and smoke bomb attacks, rifles and bayonet fighting, obstacle courses and escapes. An unusual aspect was that civilian lady drivers provided transportation. His driver, Mabel, could really "swing that buggy around," however, Jim was embarrassed by her observation of the soldiers' behavior. During ten-minute breaks, as Mabel and Jim drove down the line, the guys would unzip their britches and let it go.

Jim dealt with a few routine matters. He gave a soldier a five-day extended furlough to welcome his new baby. He conveyed the sad news of a sister's passing and helped her brother secure Red Cross funds to travel home for the funeral. He denied a soldier's pass request, concerned he would not return in time to ship out. Being AWOL was the worst crime a serviceman could commit.

With a much lighter schedule, Jim had a little time to purchase a few gifts for his children and to send some additional letters home. He sent a dress to Pie Pooh, flight caps with insignia to the boys, and a pair of leggings for Jim for his eleventh birthday. He sent his condolences to Sam's mother for the loss of her husband, a fine Kentucky gentleman, and expressed sympathy to Sam.

On February 1, 1943, Jim wrote to Ann:

"Dearest Mrs. Pooh,

I have some startling news – I've got some secret warning orders which looks like I may be going to play marbles for keeps. Everything is very hush hush and I'll let you know as things unfold, however, I honestly don't know where I am headed.

I will get orders to leave in the next day or two, so I'm packing up and getting set.

Then I may be in this country for a while, but this time the handwriting is too plain to be wrong. If James is sound in wind and limb, it's "off we go into the silver blue yonder, climbing high into the sun."

After this month's check my pay check will be $100 less per month which will go to me wherever I am and the rest to the bank, as usual. I think this is best as I might get somewhere that personal checks couldn't be cashed and it would be nice to have Uncle Sam giving me something.

Kiss the "monkey tails" for me and a million kisses for you. Remember everything will turn out gloriously in the not-too-distant future.

Your Mr. Pooh"

Jim was given a nice sendoff at a Sheppard Field farewell party. After several days of train hopping, Jim arrived in Florida. He received word that he wasn't leaving for a week.

Ann and Pie Pooh took the train to spend Valentine's Day with him. They had a splendid time with each other, enjoying the warm sunny days and walking along the boardwalk in Palm Beach.

After a pleasant visit, Ann's and Pie Pooh's departure put Jim in the doldrums. He was sad about seeing his dear wife and precious daughter unhappy about leaving him. He again questioned his decision to enlist. "At last Army life has gotten me down."

The next day his situation changed drastically. When Jim enlisted and expected to help in the states, he never thought about needing a passport. After receiving orders that he would serve as an intelligence officer, his departure was delayed for two weeks while his passport request was processed in Washington, D.C. The following interaction ensued.

Jim recalibrated and contacted Embarkation. They said, "We'll have your orders early tomorrow morning so get set."

I went over the next morning and they said, "We'll have them in half an hour. You are going in a plane full of colonels."

I said, "How about baggage?"

The captain said, "One hundred pounds – send the rest home."

"Could you give me some idea of what I should take in the way of clothes?"

His response, "No."

Mr. Pooh dashed off, bought a barracks bag, rushed down and got a second set of shots, and tore back to get his orders. When he got back the captain said, "We are all set. Have you got your passport?"

"I had my picture taken and it is over in the passport section."

"Oh," says he, "we have to send that to Washington, D.C. That's just a passport request."

Jim asked, "Would you recommend that I study Aerodrome Security, Combat Squadron Organization, Administration, Airplane Identification, Supply, desert or jungle warfare?"

He said, "Oh no – just take it easy while you can. You'll need it but it looks like a swell deal for you."

Jim joked with Ann that if he'd known sooner, he could have given his passport application to Mrs. Pooh as a secret messenger for Uncle Sam.

With all the uncertainty about his next assignment, Jim felt like he was at the center of a detective story but he felt strangely at ease about the whole thing. It was rather interesting to just take it easy and wonder whether he was going to Russia, India, Australia, Africa or South America. He didn't know if he was going to sit at a desk, in a tank, or in an airplane and get shot at, or write letters to Hitler or Hirohito. All of those decisions about his future were out of his control.

During the next three weeks, Jim stayed at Morrison Air Transport Command. Many military personnel flew between Morrison Field and India, from which they made trips to China. The trip, which was nicknamed "flying the hump" over the Himalayas Mountains, took over two weeks each way. The planes made stops in Puerto Rico, British Guinea, and Brazil before the last 1,428 miles across the ocean without refueling to Ascension Island. From there, they stopped in Liberia, then flew up the west coast of Africa and across the Sahara Desert to French Morocco in North Africa, and on to India. Military secrecy demanded that Palm Beach County's civilians had little idea of the importance of this command until after it was deactivated in 1947.

While he waited for his passport, Jim had time to write a few letters and share his experiences with his sons and encourage them to help their mother. He described big B-17 and B-24 bombers that came from all over the world. Pilots with parachutes on their backs and mechanics and grease monkeys moved on and off the field performing their duties. The pilots bought whole cases of soap or cigarettes or chocolate from the Post Exchange to give to the boys at the next stop. "They think of distance in terms of hours and not like we do as a long journey."

The young pilots seemed to enjoy their work and meeting with their friends at different ports. After listening to them talk, Jim didn't feel he would be very far from home no matter where he went. "The other side of the world isn't any further away than going across a couple of states was a generation ago." It was easy to see why these boys liked flying best. But Jim missed drilling soldiers as he was an Infantryman at heart, in spite of the wings he wore.

Jim met many interesting people who flew or fought all over the world. One soldier, based in Iceland, shared that 26 of 50 men in his outfit had died during the past year. Iceland remained neutral throughout the war, however, an Allied airbase at Reykjavik, supported the patrol of U-boats and mines during the continuous naval battle of the Atlantic and fighting in the Pacific.

The pilots seemed more interested in where to get a good drink in Natal or a tasty meal in Paris, or how the price of jewelry had gone up in India instead of what they had done or what their next job would be. Perhaps that was their way of dealing with danger and uncertainty.

During his respite, Jim went to the dog races for the first time. He bet on "Little Jimmy, Chilly Billy, and Lucky Ann" and won $5 and joked that betting on the horses might be a good job after the war. He also played a few rounds of golf. Even with the distractions, he was anxious to get to his next posting.

Jim was assigned as an intelligence officer in a Fighter Command. He had a hunch that he was going to Africa, but didn't know for sure, so he sent Ann a cartoon of the pyramids and mentioned that he might be going into the rug business. He explained the secrecy angle. Example: A General may say that he has a Captain Greene on his staff. If an enemy agent heard that comment, he could follow me. He reassured his wife. "I will tell you everything I can as things move along. I might run into Sam someday given the direction I am pointed and the physical I took. Three other men on my flight are headed to Africa, across Africa and India, respectively. I hope the war is no harder on you than it is on me. Pray that I'll do a good job – not for me, and keep the old chin up." With those sentiments, Jim was ready to head overseas to a destination yet to be determined.

Chapter 6
A Grand Adventure

The five officers climbed into a refitted, poorly heated and under-pressurized cargo plane for an extended trip with multiple stops. The interior contained no rows of seats or baggage storage. Instead, the passengers arranged themselves in a couple of chairs, leaning against luggage, and sprawled on the floor. Very soon, at about two miles up, turbulence and cold changed the scene dramatically. Everything was thrown around the cabin and the men were rolled up like balls to keep themselves warm and safe from the instability for the duration of the flight.

As he traveled to his new assignment, Jim stopped in a number of territories and countries on several continents. He seemed to enjoy the trip despite the uncomfortable time in the air. "Good food and good quarters all along the line and above all good company." The first stop on the "South Atlantic Route" was Puerto Rico, a United States territory. During World War II, it is estimated by the Department of Defense that 65,034 Puerto Ricans were drafted into the U.S. military. As the numbers increased, many soldiers were assigned to units in the Panama Canal zone and the British West Indies to replace the continental troops serving in regular Army units.

The next stop was Natal, Brazil. Brazil was the only South American nation to provide troops to the Allies. The country made significant contributions to the war effort. They sent an expeditionary force to fight alongside the Allies in the Italian campaign. The Brazilian Navy and Air Force helped the Allies in the Atlantic from 1942 until the end of the war in 1945.

A 15-hour flight across the Atlantic took Jim to Accra, on the west coast of Africa. Accra is now the capital of Ghana; at the time it was a British colony called the Gold Coast. From bases there, Allied aircraft flew missions between the United States, Europe, and the Pacific Ocean. Ghanaian colonial troops also played an important role in liberating Ethiopia from Italian control.

After landing in Ghana, the weary men disembarked from the disheveled plane. "It was rather late and a lieutenant and I were the last out of the buckets. We were assigned quarters in pre-fab barracks with enlisted personnel. It rained all evening and in the ensuing crap game we (the officers) cleaned the boys out. Sharing that experience, bars (officers' rank) mean something more than stories and ornaments." The guys fully engaged in the fun with their comrades and felt the fellowship of the group; it carried them into the next dangerous assignment. Jim's luck continued when he awoke the next day. He saw two rainbows in perfect circles and took it as a good omen.

During the layover, Jim headed into the nearest village. He was surprised that residents in every hut had American or British currency. The money's novelty had worn off because the local people didn't know how to make best use of the foreign currency. The children traded it like play money to buy chocolate bars. Jim had a practical exposure to the law of supply and demand. "I could have set up housekeeping for the price of a white undershirt." Those articles of clothing seemed to be stylish at the moment. They were scarce and could be sold for a lot of money. The ignorant could be easily exploited.

The next leg of Jim's journey, 2,222 nautical miles, entailed crossing most of the African continent to Khartoum, the capital of Sudan. Khartoum is located in a lush setting at the confluence of the White Nile flowing north from Lake Victoria and the Blue Nile flowing west from Lake Tana in Ethiopia. The Sudan Defense Forces (SDF) provided the garrison for Jalo Oasis, a quite large body of salty water in the desert, which was of strategic importance. British Military Intelligence in Cairo worked very closely with the SDF and enlisted them in numerous operations during the North African campaign. While in Khartoum, Jim reported to his family that he took time to play with lion cubs, leopards and "huffalumps" (elephants) but, he informed them, he didn't see any Pooh Bears while on safari.

The Army took no note of day or night and served meals around the clock for constant arrivals and departures, with weather playing a major role in complicating travel plans. Jim experienced such a weather delay before his flight headed to a stopover in Saudi Arabia. Again, he was at the mercy of things beyond his control and continued to adapt.

He was part of a major influx of personnel in the Middle East Theatre. The fighting against German and Italian troops in the North African Theatre was wrapping up and the next phase, a plan for taking over southern Europe, was being organized. "The long middle leg of the race was about to begin, of uncertain duration, over an undetermined course, and few doubted that new virtues would be needed: Endurance, impenitence, an obdurate will," according to Rick Atkinson in The Day of Battle.

In February 1943, command of the Eighth Army passed from the British Middle East Command to the Allied Joint Command for the Mediterranean, known as Allied Forces Headquarters (AFHQ). The entire Middle East Theatre, from Southwestern Asia to Eastern Africa, was quiet from 1943 until the end of the war. Once Germany surrendered their African campaign on May 13, 1943, the Allies maintained control of that area. The main goal now was to eliminate Italy from the Axis partnership. Jim's orders eventually took him into the North Africa region for that offensive.

After leaving Saudi Arabia, Jim's next stop was Abu Sueir, Egypt, between the Suez Canal and Cairo. Abu Sueir, built by the British before the war, was used as a military airfield by the Royal Air Force of the United Kingdom and the U.S. Air Force during the North African Campaign. Surrounding the base were hundreds of miles of some of the most fertile agricultural land in the world, the Nile Valley. As they had for hundreds of years, the Egyptians still tilled the land with traditional wooden plows and rakes pulled by buffalo, oxen, cows, camels, and donkeys. Irrigation was provided by a maze of Nile tributaries and canals. Water was distributed to the land adjacent to the canals by a variety of animal driven paddle wheel devices, dating back to the time of the Pharaohs. The canals were also major thoroughfares for hundreds of large, single sail cargo boats used for transporting goods throughout the delta.

At Abu Sueir, Jim stayed in permanent barracks where the beds were lined up like an infirmary. Slowly he was learning to adjust to a new way of life. For example, he fetched hot water from the kitchen with his helmet for a morning shave. He commented that he was adding a few pounds due to the delicious G.I. food, served on personal mess kits. These items consisted of a divided metal plate with a top section that could be used as a skillet for cooking and utensils. "The Old Gent (Uncle Sam) with the white goatee never forgets to feed his nephews."

While at Abu Sueir, he engaged in intelligence work for the British, as confirmed by his orders from England. His uniform as an intelligence officer camouflaged him somewhat. "I'll now draw 'Battle Dress' which consists of a British uniform with a little tab on the shoulder with U.S. on it. They say the reason is that some of our uniforms are too much like the Germans and it avoids confusion."

Jim described his detective work for the British in a letter to his family, "I still find fascinating things for a prying Pooh Bear to stick his nose. I think I am quite safe so long as no booby traps catch me. If I don't write at times don't be alarmed, I may be tripping around checking out the relics and not able to write or I can't say anything."

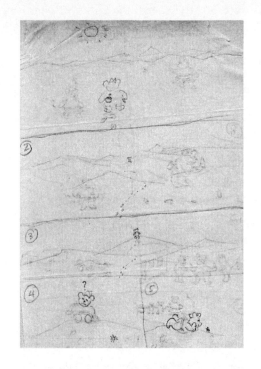

Officers who were not flying had the chore of censoring outgoing mail. Jim and the other officers even censored each other's mail. The assembled armed with razor blades, read the missives, cut out any sensitive military parts, and resealed the envelopes.

In his spare time, Jim joined a few other officers for a camel ride around the ancient ruins. His camel, named Beauty, protested at being made to get up but trotted away once she was standing. Another day found him touring a site where captured equipment was being studied by ordinance men. Occasionally, a movie, such as *Casablanca*, *Wake Island*, and *Six Gentlemen from West Point*, was shown in the evening. The movies were on reels and projected on to an outside screen. A few early arrivers sat on old oil drums but most men stood.

Jim really enjoyed "chewing the fat" with other officers who had traveled and fought around the world. Conversations with many men who had been in combat since the beginning of the war shed collective light on their perceptions. It seemed the more entrenched they were in warfare, the less they knew of world dynamics, particularly the restrictions and rationing in the States, as they were very isolated from the news. They mostly lived in temporary situations with little radio reception or printed material.

One soldier commented, "I bet if I got to New York, I could get a second-hand car and drive to Oklahoma."

Another enlisted man chimed in, "Shucks, I'd have a date with my girl every night; she only lives 80 miles away."

A husband chuckled, "Hell, if my wife doesn't get a pair of shoes a month, she'll be over here shortly."

A more thoughtful remark, "Is there anything we can send the folks at home?"

As time went on, he found the latter view to be more and more the case as they had better access to the news from the States. The men became concerned about the hardships facing their families and friends at home.

Jim ventured into Cairo as part of his acclimation to the region. Middle East cultural differences were immediately apparent during the 80-mile trip along the Sweet Water Canal. "Sweet Water" was a misnomer. Local people would use the canal to defecate, bathe, and wash clothes, even though it was the main source of their drinking water.

While in Cairo, Jim rode on a streetcar, took a bus, and sailed in a little boat along the Nile during his exploration. He observed several ethnic groups and thought the children were very handsome with their nice smiles. He concluded that people in this neck of the woods wore nightgowns or bathrobes as their native dress so that, at their convenience, they could lie down and sleep in the city, a village, or in the open country. Along about noon, the women and children took baths in front of their houses. He thought that the men considered it sissy to bathe, based on their appearance and smell. However, in general he found the native people cheerful and remarkable "to keep going on a gallon of sand and a couple of quarts of stories."

On the other hand, he had a different theory about the work animals. "I'm beginning to believe the camels have lost their sense of humor in the last few thousand years as they are the sole support of everybody and have to keep their noses to the grindstone." He found a great discrepancy between what he saw and how the movies interpreted this part of the world. The movies and magazines didn't portray either the poverty and deprivation or the friendliness and community spirit with which he came in contact.

One Sunday, Jim and another captain went to an Anglican church service where they were the only two white people present. Regardless, the similarities in the liturgy were so familiar they felt at home and sang along. The congregation greeted them warmly.

After the service, they wandered through town. Jim found that shopping was a negotiating ritual. If he spent a little time, he could get what he wanted at the right price. He played the bargaining game and found a pocketbook for Ann because he'd noticed when they were in Florida that hers was patched up with paper clips. There was also entertainment at the market. A monkey thumbing his nose at Mussolini and bowing to Uncle Sam while marching and dancing caught his attention.

After a "cook's tour" to several bases, a little detective work, and adjustment to a dusty, dry environment, Jim joined one of the best outfits in the Middle East. General Marshall organized the 376th Heavy Bombardment group with four squadrons which was part of the first consolidated B-24 Liberator Group to be based in the European Theater. The Group engaged in combat as part of the Ninth, Twelfth and Fifteenth Air Forces in the Egypt/Libya and Italian Campaigns.

Jim began his assignment with the Group by leading a convoy of ground crews on an 800-mile trip from Abu Sueir, Egypt to Soluch, Libya, 30 miles southeast, down the coast from Benghazi. They left Abu Sueir just in time, as the base was bombed shortly after the troop train left. The tree-lined road along the Mediterranean coast took them through rolling hills with green pastures that were once pretty little farm communities. Now the landscape was mostly a junkman's hunting ground after the recent battles. "This whole continent is a collector's paradise with a kind of Fourth of July backdrop." However, collecting souvenirs subjected one to life-threatening danger due to land mines. Lecturing to the troops about safety wasn't necessary after the convoy saw a Sudanese soldier killed. On the way to Soluch, they sped past a number of British convoys who were obeying speed regulations, unlike the Americans.

Before the war, Soluch was an Italian outpost consisting of a few narrow streets lined with single story stucco and stone buildings. Olive, oleander, and willow-like trees provided a modicum of shade along the lanes. The shopkeepers slaughtered and dressed lamb, goats, and mutton outside and sold the meat in their fly-ridden shops. A crier in a picturesque minaret called worshippers to Muslim prayers five times daily. The Scnussi, a faction of the Muslim religion, were severely oppressed by the Italian conquerors of Libya in earlier times. The infuriated natives got revenge by relaying every move by the Italians and Germans to the British and Americans.

Soluch natives were true nomads, roaming the barren land to feed their flocks of sheep.

Their encampments consisted of several individual family tents laced together to form one common roof. To Westerners, conditions seemed unsanitary and crowded. Jim wrote: "Lean-tos the size of cow stalls had about 200 inhabitants. In the dim light, you couldn't tell a bundle of rags from inhabitants. The women silently sit in corners and only show their eyes. The children scuttle through shell holes in the walls and undrained sewage ditches. Old ammunition serves as treasure chests in which they keep rags, rotten meat, broken knives, grain, bottles and eggs. I got a handful of flies when I poked into one box and I hate to think of the germs. I can't figure out how they don't die."

Soon after their arrival at Soluch, the group moved to Berka 2, located four miles from Benghazi and yards from the Mediterranean Sea. When possible, Jim ended his day swimming in the sea or building sandcastles on the beach.

He was reminded of his memorable visits to Rehoboth Beach with his relatives as a young person, and later as an adult. He reflected on how fortunate he was and how much he wanted his children and grandchildren to continue to have the life that he experienced. It reinforced his purpose and determination to be part of the Allied war effort.

The squadrons set up their white, 16 feet square tents among date, palm and fig trees. The tents, serving as bomb shelters, sat over a hole about two feet deep, giving three occupants five feet of height and plenty of room to accommodate their luggage. Drainage ditches were dug around the tents to prevent flooding. The recessed floor provided the same shelter as a slit trench. These shelters were necessary as the Axis flew daily reconnaissance planes over the area. German bombing raids from operations in Sicily and Crete were a constant threat.

The layout of the interior of the tents was as varied as the imagination and resourcefulness of the crews that lived in them. Most of the tents started out with bare dirt floors, which guaranteed a housekeeping problem whenever the wind blew in any strength. Woven mats bartered from the Senussi provided some measure of relief. The Arab bazaar shopkeepers sold pressurized gasoline stoves similar in design to Coleman stoves. The men used them to ward off the desert night chill and to warm snacks – until the sand plugged up the stoves and caused small explosions. After those incidents, the stoves were quickly banned.

Lieutenant Madden and Jim hauled marble for their flooring from the Benghazi rubble to create a marble "palace." There, despite the elegant floor, Jim had to use candlelight as the main source of lighting while writing letters home to his family, reminding them how much he missed them. "I have the littles' pictures pinned up on the tent walls smiling at me. I'll be glad when I get back to you all! It's what I live for."

Insects were constant companions and a persistent menace. Lethal scorpions, as poisonous as rattlesnakes, crawled into shoes. On the other hand, the animals were playful. "The cute little braying jackasses wake me up in the morning. I fed a lump of precious sugar to a baby and it tried to follow me into the tent. Its mother called and it galloped away. I hope our children are as obedient," Jim wrote.

During the move and establishment of the new base, sanitation reached a new low. There was always a shortage of fresh water as it had to be hauled from a British supply point three miles away. Poor mess hall sanitation and the bucket latrine system contributed to the unhealthy conditions. As a result, many of the men contracted intestinal maladies. Several changes solved the problem. Separate mess facilities were established for each squadron allowing for improved hygiene. Bucket latrines were replaced with an oil drum pit system. Even so, a shortage of lumber precluded construction of anything approaching enclosed toilets.

Another major component of camp life was the ever present fine reddish sand. The talcum-like powder permeated clothes and was an unwelcome ingredient in food. Frequently the sand was deposited by wind swirls in the tents. "The Texas sandstorms are like Pie Pooh's sandbox compared to the African sandstorms." The sand was a constant problem for the bomber engines, reducing their service life from 300 hours to 60 hours. The maintenance crews toiled endlessly replacing parts in oppressive heat to keep the camouflage pink B-24s flying.

After getting settled at Berka 2, Jim saw the war's impact on Benghazi. The seemingly happy and well-fed Italian war prisoners worked detail instead of fighting. Jim wrote, "It must have been beautiful once. Our own outfit contributed to what it is now. It makes a man realize that anything is better than to let war get to your own shores. We are just screwballs if we don't go in for compulsory military training and an adequate defense force when this is over. Getting caught with our pants down was folly once, but would be criminal a second time. We need to be ready to smack them down quickly when somebody in Ding Dong a million miles away hops on his neighbor even at the sacrifice of thousands of men so that something like this will never get started and all disputes will be brought to a court of nations."

Jim, like many Americans, believed in the need for international cooperation and a collective group of world representatives to address issues that threatened to lead to war. In 1945, representatives of 50 countries met in San Francisco at the United Nations Conference on International Organization to draw up the United Nations Charter. The purpose of the United Nations was to save succeeding generations from war, to reaffirm faith in fundamental human rights, to establish conditions under which justice and respect for the obligations arising from treaties and other source of international law can be maintained, and to promote social progress. These developments grew, at least in part, from realizations such as Jim expressed during his time in Libya.

Meanwhile the activity in North Africa continued. The 376th Group was able to become independent of British resources and more highly organized with the influx of personnel from the states. Late in the afternoon, crew members checked the bulletin boards to see if they were on a mission the next day. The schedules would include the planes, crews, and position in formation. There was a timetable for breakfast, briefing, and boarding trucks for transport to the aircraft dispersal area.

There was no mention of the target, but crew members became adept at guessing the target based on the bombs to be carried. Fragmentation bombs meant an airfield, 2,000 pounders generally implied docks or a ferry terminal, and 500-pound general purpose bombs might be headed for marshalling yards or convoy ships. If a fuel tank was added to the bomb bay, the crews knew they were going for a long ride.

Before sunrise, personnel headed to the mess hall. Combat attire consisted of a few layers for warmth, fleece-lined jackets, inflatable life vests, goggles, hats with earflaps, and dog tags. After breakfast, the officers and crew broke out to get specific instructions. The Group Operations Officer discussed the nature of the target and its significance to the Axis war effort, the route to and from the target, and the formation. Jim, as an intelligence officer, pointed out the general position of enemy guns and fighter bases and made an educated guess about what opposition could be expected in the target area. Finally, he presented a synopsis of the ground war based on his briefing from Col. Compton and his contacts in other parts of the world. The weather officer gave information on cloud formation, winds and atmospheric pressure in the target areas. The format of these briefings remained essentially unchanged for the remainder of the war.

Almost daily, the combat crews faced the daunting ordeal of flying into the flak-filled skies. The expression, "heavy and accurate anti-aircraft fire" means nothing to someone who has never experienced it, but for the men flying into that man-made hell of hot steel day after day, those words caused an unthinkable amount of agony and tragedy. The crews always had to go into the battle confident that they would win.

The 376th Bombardment Group allowed the British to experiment with homing pigeons as a survival aid to crews who were faced with ditching in the Mediterranean Sea. The popular theory was that homing pigeons were motivated to return to their familiar surroundings, mates, and food sources.

Each bird had a small capsule attached to one leg containing a form on which a crew in distress could write relevant data. Although the "Pigeon Project" lasted several months, there were no recorded occasions when the birds were used in an emergency.

The Ninth Combat Camera Unit (9CCU) was an unheralded but vital detachment which supported the 376th Group in recording damaged targets. The unit was formed in Culver City, California, as part of the First Motion Picture Unit composed largely of actors, technicians, and cameraman recruited from the movie industry. The Unit, consisting of 32 cameramen and technicians, reported on December, 1942. The role of the 9CCU was to provide a cameraman on each mission to record target damage. The cameramen shared all the risks with the air crews and lost 23 members. They received little recognition.

Jim shared a few thoughts with his sons.

"Lots of very interesting things happen, as you might expect, in an outfit of heavy bombers but we are not allowed to tell anything because the enemy might find out too much about us. You might read in the paper about our raids, but we don't know enough about what's going on to know what can and can't be said, so we say nothing.

"There are certainly a fine lot of boys in the outfit and they are just as modest and quiet about their exploits as if they had been shooting at sparrows with bb guns. It makes me feel good to know that you are the same sort of American boys who are polite and nice but who can fight so well and never boast about it.

"This would be a lovely place to camp if there was a nice spring nearby and no flies, fleas, centipedes, or scorpions to bother you. Also, it's a bit chilly at night and a bit hot all day."

With the proximity to Ninth Bomber Command headquarters in Benghazi, the 376th Group was visited frequently by both British and American VIPs and other dignitaries. Jim led a parade honoring the King of Greece. Several USO entertainment troupes, including comedian Jack Benny, visited and put on shows at the open-air theatre where the audience of servicemen watched from seats made from oil drums. The soldiers had to laugh whenever possible to keep their wits about them because they experienced so much pain from injuries and loss.

Near the end of April, the 376th learned of a concentration of German fighter planes in Bari, Italy, on the east side of the Italian boot. All available bombers, 35 planes, participated in the mission. The surprise raid destroyed a hanger, 18 fighter planes, and severely damaged 125 planes. All planes returned unscathed. On the evening of May 1, the Germans demonstrated that they could still retaliate for the Allies' ever-expanding bombing raids across the Mediterranean Sea. Just after dusk, the air raid siren sounded and the lights went out at Berka 2. Tentative heads emerged from the slit trenches to witness a dazzling pyrotechnic display lasting more than 40 minutes over a British convoy outside Benghazi harbor.

During the last weeks before the Axis surrendered in North Africa, the 376th missions were directed toward keeping up the pressure on Rommel's dwindling supply lines to Tunisia. The ground war in North Africa formally ended on May 13, 1943, with the surrender of the last elements of the Afrika Korps bottled up at Cape Bon, Tunisia, about 1,200 miles along the coast northwest of Benghazi. At the end of their resistance in Africa, 250,000 Axis troops entered Allied POW camps.

With a brief lull in fighting, Jim took a moment to share his observations about desert animal life while he was "Alert Officer" headquartered in a shell of a shattered house. He described little timid lizards, like chameleons, that scuttled around the walls, while large, ugly, vicious lizards attacked sticks. Small desert porcupines ball up and roll down a sand dune when frightened. The harmless spiders are as big as mice. According to his neighbors, Jim attracted a spotted snake at his tent. "The snake probably discovered my collection of kangaroo mice, gray mice and blue mice. I don't truck with the black mice as they make a mess and smell bad."

He observed large black ants marching across the sand like foragers bringing seeds and dropping them in holes, only the hulls left in their supply dumps. He likened their behavior to the troops, "We leave behind numerable tin cans, tin hats, gas masks, canteens, clothing and everything conceivable from toothbrushes to tanks."

Suddenly he heard a burst of machine gun fire and realized it was a few boys breaking the monotony. Next, he heard a chicken, and upset his chair bursting into the moonlight to catch it, to no avail. Chickens were valuable and if he had caught it, he would have traded it for a few cigarettes. Jim wrote, "I'm down to my last pack of cigarettes. I believe I can make it, thinking of (George) Washington at Valley Forge." He appreciated not being in the freezing cold.

With the end of the Desert War, the 376th turned its attention to neutralizing a network of German airfields dotting the Italian peninsula at Foggia, Grottaglie, and Taranto. The bombers attacked the airfields at Comiso and Gerbini, vital refueling points for enemy transport planes to ferry supplies between Italy and North Africa. As an intelligence officer, Jim went on several reconnaissance flights and though it was against protocol, he substituted on a few bombing missions, mostly while in Africa.

Late in the evening of June 14, 1943, the 376th got a taste of the ground war. A Senussi sheep herder alerted the base that approximately 50 enemy paratroopers dropped near Benghazi. Their mission was to destroy or sabotage American and British planes. Most of the men were captured quickly without opposition. However, for two weeks, a few stalwarts killed two guards, blew up two B-24s, and destroyed eight RAF Wellington bombers before surrendering. Jim didn't get much information when he interrogated the prisoners.

Many German raids on the recaptured ports of Tobruk and Benghazi were originating from Greece. The 376th responded with pinpoint accuracy destroying all the structures, enemy aircraft and cratering the runway, deterring further operations at Salonika in the northwestern corner of the island. Three days later, an equally successful raid decimated another German airfield Kalamaki, near Athens.

July's major focus was Sicily and southern Italy. Air Force commanders believed that airpower should concentrate on airfields and supply lines. Intelligence reported a large aggregation of Germany's highest-ranking officers were meeting at an ancient summer resort on the east coast, near Taormina, Sicily. All 216 bombs hit on or very near their targets. A Luftwaffe commander wrote, "…a turning point had come and that we were on the road to final defeat."

Simultaneously, the 376th systematically knocked out a network of heavily used airfields surrounding Bari, Italy, on the southeastern coast. The 376th made many missions to Messina, a vital Axis supply port on the southwestern coast, before putting it out of business. Naples, another major port, required many attempts before it was shut down.

The decision for an aerial attack on Rome was issued jointly by Prime Minister Churchill and President Roosevelt. Churchill insisted, "No objective can compete with the capture of Rome." Considerable preparation went into this assault. The night before, planes flew over, dropping leaflets telling the citizens when and where there would be bombing. The Vatican and other prohibited areas were outlined with smoke pots as accuracy was critical. Catholic crew members were given the option to withdraw from the mission in case they had qualms about attacking the papal city, but no man did. Nineteen 376th bombers joined 272 planes for the three-hour attack and returned safely.

In late July, the attack on the Littorio marshalling yards, a major transportation complex, on the east side of Rome, made worldwide headlines. The massive strike left the railyards in shambles without any damage outside the target area. Tired of the war, peasants along the route waved encouragement to the bombers. The Allies now had a foothold on the underside of Europe and were beginning the long push northward.

While Jim was in the midst of war, the Greene family was living in a dramatically changed environment. What had formerly been a southern city of grace and charm, Washington, D.C. became a frenzied capital of the world, inundated with relocated wartime workers and visitors. Ann was challenged with the increase in traffic and other complications. She did her best to continue her normal routines, like taking the children to Easter services at Christ Episcopal Church in Georgetown, where she and Jim were married, and Jim's family had been members for generations. The congregation prayed for the well-being of all those serving in the military and the boys thought of their father.

While having lunch with their grandparents, the boys talked about how much they missed their dad, his sense of humor and his stories. Jimmy and Billy mentioned a few friends who had lost family members. Their grandfather responded, "Your father will return and have lots more stories to tell." He reminded them to think all was well until they knew otherwise. The boys left their grandparents' home with big hugs and smiles on their faces.

Jimmy and Billy welcomed warmer weather so they could play pick-up baseball in a nearby vacant lot and ride their bikes around the neighborhood. They were members of baseball teams and played tennis at the Recreation Center. The family did their part for the war effort. The boys continued their paper routes, using their money to buy war bonds. They sold war stamps and started collecting aluminum and scrap metal for recycling. Ann planted her first Victory Garden of vegetables and volunteered at the Red Cross. In celebration of Mother's Day, she hosted a luncheon and bridge for several VMI widows.

While Jim suffered from a touch of typhus fever in Africa, summer brought the measles to the Greene home. Mrs. Pooh nursed them back to good health. Jim wrote with ironic encouragement, "Measles, whooping cough and chicken pox are finished now. You only have to have mumps, typhoid, pneumonia, and two wars and you will catch up with Daddy."

Jim sent money orders home monthly after paying for his meals and any necessary clothing. One month, he missed. "I got involved in a drinking spree with two British, one Australian, and one Canadian officer. It was accidental but all in the good cause of cementing world relations." He summed up his financial situation in the following English nursery rhyme.

I've got sixpence
Jolly, jolly sixpence
I've got sixpence to last me all my life
I've got two pence to spend

And two pence to lend
And two pence to send home to my wife--poor wife.
No cares have I to grieve me
No pretty little girls to deceive me
I'm happy as a lark believe me
As we go rolling, rolling home
By the light of the silvery moon
Happy is the day when we line up for our pay
As we go rolling, rolling home.

On a lighter note, the 376th public information section promoted a contest to come up with a nickname for the Group. The winning name was the "Liberandos," coined from the words, liberator and commando. The emblem was a yellowed winged sphinx representing the Middle East set upon a terra cotta red, signifying the desert. The bomb in the upper right identified the mission of the Group and was set in a blue background symbolizing the African sky.

The end of July found the Liberandos preparing for the greatest aerial assault in history.

Chapter 7
The Assault

At this point in early 1943, Jim was included in the planning for most missions of the 376th Group. He was instrumental in gathering intelligence and aided in developing strategy for the attacks. He was helpful in configuring crews as he made it a point to know his comrades and their skills. His work was vital because the officers constantly reiterated the importance of accuracy in bombing targets so as to minimize human loss.

In late June, olive drab B-24 bombers from three groups of the Eighth Air Force in England joined the dull pink planes from the resident 376th and 98th Groups. The aircraft were assigned to satellite fields around Benghazi. The five groups immediately began working together and practicing low-level flying missions. However, they did not know the location of the mission.

Ground crews added two 400-gallon fuel tanks to the forward bomb bays of each bomber. The amount of fuel needed suggested a mission that would exceed ten hours in length. A potentially dangerous problem with this arrangement was an explosion if the empty fuel tanks were hit. Ground crews worked around the clock making adjustments to prevent this hazard. Their work was critical to the assault.

General Lewis H. Brereton and five group commanders spent July planning Operation Tidal Wave. Royal Air Force Squadron Leader Charles Barwell was brought in to provide additional bomber training. He taught the crews where to aim to hit the enemy who was firing at them. An effective leader, he devised simple rules, taught them well, and flew on the mission with the men.

On July 24, after a month of training, the combat crew officers were assembled in a closed "War Room." They were finally told that the target was the Ploesti Oil refineries in eastern Rumania. On the last day of July, the men of the 376th were poised to participate in one of the most daring missions of World War II.

The concept of this mission to Ploesti developed in January 1943 at the highest level – the Casablanca Conference in Morocco. President Roosevelt, Prime Minister Churchill and the chief war planners of the Allied nations were in attendance. The land invasion of Europe was the main purpose of the meeting. An attack across the English Channel was postponed. Operation Tidal Wave, the attack on Ploesti, became a footnote to the invasion plan, albeit an important one.

It was estimated that a successful bombing raid against Ploesti could deny Hitler one third of his fuel production and, thereby shorten the war by six months. While the Allies had world-wide sources of oil to fuel the engines of war, Germany's only source was the synthetic oil production within its homeland and the crude oil products available in European countries under Hitler's control. Ploesti, Rumania had the largest production capacity in Europe outside of Russia.

Operation Tidal Wave emerged from the Casablanca Conference as a good idea in theory but one that seemed almost impossible to achieve in reality. The Allied High Command issued secret orders to General Brereton that his 9th Air Force should bomb Ploesti in the interim between the end of the North Africa campaign, estimated to be only months away, and the subsequent invasion of Sicily. "Tidal Wave was one of the few instances in WWII in which the High Command handed down a major task to a theater commander without asking him if it was feasible," noted war correspondents James Dugan and Carroll Stewart.

The target was NOT Ploesti, a city inhabited by 100,000 Rumanian citizens. Many of these civilians were opposed to the German occupation and privately supported the Allied advances. Instead, the targets were the nearby Axis oil refineries.

Among the myriad challenges to Tidal Wave was the selection of targets for the raid. The city was ringed with rail lines that connected more than a dozen large refineries, the lifeblood of the local economy and significant fuel for Hitler's war. The challenge was to strike the refineries across a five-mile circumference without any errant bombs falling on the civilian population. This factor, more than any other, precipitated Colonel Smart's initial concept for a low-level mission.

While attending the Trident Conference in Washington, D.C. in May 1943, with Roosevelt and Churchill, Colonel J.E. Smart presented his plans for a low-level bombing raid. Again, the Ploesti attack was overshadowed by the larger concerns of Operation Husky, the invasion of Sicily. General Marshall noted that even "a fairly successful attack on Ploesti would stagger Berlin." General Eisenhower approved the mission.

Colonel Smart returned to England to plan the attack. He had to convince General Brereton and General U.G. Ent that the B-24s should bomb at rooftop level. An element of surprise and extreme bombing accuracy could only be achieved by low altitude attacks. This strategy was especially dangerous for the aircraft because they could be shot down more easily by the Axis support on land. Smart hoped that as many as 200 B-24 Liberators would be available for Operation Tidal Wave. It was optimistic to think this many planes would be available to carry out this attack.

Nevertheless, 200 planes constituted too small a force to strike all the refineries that circled Ploesti. Accordingly, seven primary oil production facilities were selected. The 1,100 mile, high altitude flights of long duration would expose aircraft and crews to hazards of interception long before reaching the target. As a result, the formation was plotted to approach the city from the west because there was less enemy opposition and it created more of an element of surprise since they were flying from the south.

By mid-1943, major increases in anti-aircraft weapons around the perimeter of the refineries were secured by the enemy. These weapons proved that Axis forces appreciated the importance of safeguarding "Hitler's Jewel of the Balkans." Germans manned approximately 240 88mm guns, plus several smaller caliber weapons were placed on ridges, towers, and bridges, with some hidden in haystacks. Railroad trains with large armaments were positioned on the north and south sides of the city. Radar and several hundred barrage balloons were set up in all four quadrants. One hundred German fighter planes were situated on nine surrounding airfields with support available from airfields in Greece.

On July 31, General Brereton visited Bomber Command Headquarters and talked to the five group commanders and combat crews at each base. He exhorted the crews to "devastate" the refinery complex, pointing out that to do so would significantly shorten the war. He told them that the mission could accomplish in one day what ground forces would take a year to do.

As darkness fell over the Libyan Desert, General Brereton's inspiring words could not push away the doubts and fears of 1,700 men tasked with this mission. General Ent's 50% casualty estimate and denial of his request to alter the plan were still on Kane's mind. "If nobody comes back, the results will be worth the cost."

While plans were being made at higher levels, Jim was busy shuffling crews throughout the night, a task complicated by a bout of dysentery that had stricken a third of the men at Benghazi earlier in the week. Despite the illness, only two men didn't fly. The ground crews managed to make three more bombers flight ready for a total of 178 aircraft. The welcomed news necessitated additional volunteers to man the planes. Awaiting the next day's mission, some flight crews remained awake during the long hours of that Saturday night talking to each other, writing letters, or arranging their personal belongings to be sent home should they not return. Others sought out comfort from the chaplains.

On August 1, 1943, known as Black Sunday, a total of 178 aircraft were prepared to depart on the Tidal Wave mission, a remarkable feat considering the harsh and primitive conditions in the desert to which the personnel and airplanes were subjected. Operation Tidal Wave may have been the most thoroughly planned and intricately briefed air mission in history, and it was to be led by what was probably the most experienced leadership ever assembled.

Despite all this planning, the devil was in the unexpected.

Early Sunday morning a man-made dust storm generated by the turning propellers of 712 engines engulfed Benghazi. One of the last of the Liberandos developed problems as it lifted off and turned back to make an emergency landing. Striking a pole, the bomber crashed, killing all but two members of its eight-member crew. These were the first casualties. Before Black Sunday ended, there would be many more. Jim got an early start making arrangements for his fallen comrades, notifying their families, and preparing to send their personal items home.

The first two groups, out of five bomber groups, flew across the Mediterranean Sea for three hours, passing the enemy-held island of Corfu, Greece, and forged ahead to climb the 9,000-foot Pindes Range in northern Greece, continuing onward at an altitude of 11,000 feet. Due to the critical need to maintain strict radio silence, mission leader General Ent and pilot Colonel Keith Compton dared not verify that all of the bombers were still moving steadily toward Ploesti. Mechanical failures forced five Liberators to turn back to Africa and two bombers were lost at sea in route. They could only hope the remaining three groups were following.

General Ent thought that the most important aspect of completing this mission and returning home alive consisted of the element of surprise, and he maintained that belief. He and the other Allied leaders didn't know that the Germans already knew they were coming. Unfortunately, a spotter on the island of Corfu notified the Germans of a large number of airplanes crossing the Albanian coast and heading northeast.

A deadly firestorm would be waiting for them. On this day, upward of 200 Axis fighters were in the vicinity of Ploesti, manning anti-aircraft guns that ringed the city limits to protect the refineries. Well-trained German gunners heard the sounds of the air raid warning sirens and rushed to their stations, ready to rain death on the Americans headed toward them.

Each of the five bomber sections was assigned to attack one or more of seven oil refinery complexes. Compton's Liberandos were leading to bomb Target White 1 (Romana Americana) on the east side of the city. Meanwhile Colonel Addison Baker's *Flying Circus* would divide into two attacking forces to bomb Target White 2 (Concordia Vega) and Target White 3 (Unirea Sepranta) which lay on either side of Compton's target. John Kane's *Pyramidiers* were to hit Target White 4 (Astra Romana) while Leon Johnson's *Eight Balls* split up to hit Target White 5 (Columbia Aquila) on the southwest side of the city and Target Blue at Brazi five miles south. The trailing group, Colonel Jack Wood's *Sky Scorpions*, were ordered to turn north to attack Target Red at Campina, 18 miles away.

Due to a landmark miscalculation, the lead wave turned south and found themselves 20 miles southwest of the entrance point on the road leading to the Rumanian capital of Bucharest. By the time the mistake was corrected and the formation of 25 large bombers was headed north, the ground fire had begun, and enemy fighters were moving in to join the fray.

Baker's 32 Liberators of the *Flying Circus* struck the two briefed targets, Target White 2 and Target White 3 east of Ploesti. In less than ten minutes, all of the 32 bombers flooded the south side of Ploesti with smoke and flame. Compton's Liberandos were no longer lined up to cross the city from the west to attack the original assigned target. Instead, they decided to lead the 26 Liberators in an attack on Target White 4 south of the city.

The ferocity of the enemy ground fire and the obvious devastation to the west convinced General Ent that the mission was irreparably broken. He ordered the formation to break off and strike targets of opportunity. Most of the bombers veered east beyond the heaviest enemy ground fire, dropping their bombs on smaller storage facilities in the plains beyond the refineries. Major Norman Appold and the Liberandos and Colonel Joseph Pott's *Traveling Circus* hit Target White 2. Kane's *Pyramidiers* approached a surprising sign of flames rising from their target. They continued on course to destroy Europe's largest producer of oil. Behind Kane, the *Eight Balls* attacked the burning Target White 5 and the refinery at Brazi.

Without warning, the skies turned even deadlier. During the early stages of the alert, German General Alfred Gerstenberg dispatched specially outfitted trains to travel on the tracks, normally used for transporting fuel, surrounding the refineries. These train cars hid massive guns and once the sides were open, German gunners were in perfect position to track the bombers before the pilots realized what was happening. However, the fearless pilots continued with the mission.

Target Blue suffered 100% damage inflicted by 21 airships without a single loss. Four of the six assigned targets were awash in flame. Colonel Jack Wood's *Sky Scorpions*, (assigned the title "tail end Charlie" because their target was 18 miles north of the other targets), totally destroyed Target Red.

In all, 89 of 163 bombers from the five bomb groups that reached their target made it back to Benghazi. Near sundown, after 13 hours in the air, the toll stood at 41 bombers lost in action over the target and enemy territory, eight interned in Turkey, and five crashed, for a total loss of 54 bombers and 540 men. Only 33 Liberators were pronounced "fit to fly" the next day. The casualties among the 1,726 men who flew into hell were heartrending. Nearly a third of the crews failed to return, with more than 300 known dead and 140 captured. Of those who did make it home, 440 fighters were wounded.

Help for the wounded came from unexpected places. Princess Catherine Caradja lived about ten miles from Ploesti and saw a plane crash in her nearby open field. She quickly gathered servants and farm hands and attended to the crew. She took them home and protected them, refusing to turn them over to the Germans.

For a few days after the attack, Jim, as an intelligence officer, flew to assess the damage with his tentmate and photographer, Lieutenant L.J. Madden, in the *Eight Balls*, one of the few undamaged planes. Jim saw the destruction and gained valuable information for planning future missions. He was impressed with the target accuracy. In order to alleviate worry and for military security reasons, he downplayed the significance of the mission and his role when he wrote to Ann, "Around the first part of August I missed writing for a couple of days when I went on a rather extended tour of foreign parts."

After analyzing the destruction, the leadership in Washington, D.C. determined that, in less than 30 minutes, the Axis lost over 40% of its critical oil production. Capacity dropped from 9,235,000 tons to 5,300,000 tons. Thus, future refinery production of high-octane fuels would barely suffice to keep the Luftwaffe aircraft in the air, even temporarily. General Gerstenberg was acutely aware that while the bombs had been falling over Ploesti that day, the Allies had painted a bull's eye over his domain. He was certain they would be back.

General Gerstenberg was right. It was obvious that a single raid on Ploesti was not sufficient in the long run. Due to the heavy losses, no more low-level attacks were planned. Future strikes on this priority target would wait until bases in Italy could be established.

Eighth months later, on April 5, 1944, the Liberandos returned to Ploesti with 200 other B-24s and B-17s. This mission signaled a continuous aerial siege against Ploesti for five months. Oil production continued to dwindle and finally stopped in August 1944. The cost to the Allies was high. In addition to the Tidal Wave losses, 223 B-24s and B-17s were lost. Over 2,600 crewmen were killed or captured while hundreds more were wounded.

Many decorations for heroism were conferred for the Ploesti Mission on August 1, 1943. Five Congressional Medals of Honor were awarded. Fourteen other mission participants received Distinguished Service Crosses or Silver Stars for special acts of courage and leadership. Tidal Wave crewmen were individually awarded the Distinguished Flying Cross or the Air Medal. Ann sent Jim articles from the Washington, D.C. papers. He posted them for the soldiers to see the recognition for their accomplishments.

Jim spent much of August focused on Ploesti tragedies. He worked to locate all the crewmembers who didn't return and gave as accurate as possible information to family members. He sent the injured home and buried those who returned but didn't survive the mission. He helped the squadron regroup for their next missions.

In September, Jim readied his squadron to relocate from Berka 2 in Tunisia to San Pancrazio, Italy, for the remainder of the war. Although the end was not in sight, operations would not face the same obstacles. The bombers would be almost 500 miles closer to Ploesti and other targets in Europe and the Balkans. Flights would be shorter and less fatiguing. Fighter escorts could provide protection all the way to and from targets.

Chapter 8
A Long Hike

Though the Liberandos flew a number of high-altitude missions, it took some time for them to reorganize after Ploesti. Bombers needed to be repaired and replaced in the unforgiving desert in the middle of summer. Due to the heavy losses, a new contingent of personnel arrived to replenish the squadrons. Soldiers had to adapt to the difficult living conditions.

A major event took place on August 17, 1943. The Axis surrendered Sicily with 100,000 prisoners to the Allies. Twelve thousand enemy soldiers were killed in the effort to take this territory. It took six years to contradict Mussolini's admonition, "It would be a nameless folly for anyone to invade the island." With the Sicilian campaign over, the Allies accelerated attacks on Italian tactical targets in anticipation of invading the mainland of the "Boot of Italy."

Just two weeks later, another major and even more significant event took place on September 3, 1943. Italy formally surrendered to the Allies. General Dwight D. Eisenhower delayed the official announcement for five days until September 8th to prevent the Germans from occupying Italian defensive positions before the American Fifth Army could move forward through Salerno on the Amalfi coast. He knew that the Germans anticipated the Italian surrender and had confiscated 80% of the weapons of Italian divisions on duty throughout the Middle East Theater. Only nine divisions on the islands of Corsica and Sardinia were allowed to surrender directly to the Allies. News of the capitulation prompted Allied-supporting Yugoslav guerrillas to unilaterally disarm ten Italian Army divisions in the Balkans and confiscate their munitions and supplies.

By the summer of 1943, the war was wearing on Ann and Jim, as expressed in their communications. Ann's loss of weight, graying hair, and weariness were evident in photographs she sent to Jim. She was exhausted from caring for the children and other responsibilities at home under wartime restrictions. In depressed times, she wondered how long she could endure. She worried about Jim when she read the news of the Liberandos' activities without knowing how it impacted him. Sometimes her fears came across as irritations. Like most wives who remained at home, she feared the worst for her husband. Her constant thoughts were – *Was Jim well? Would he survive?*

Jim occasionally expressed his frustrations, and that did not sit well with Ann. "I agree with you that it is a little humiliating to continue as a captain when I have the responsibilities of a major. I move convoys, pull on defense when attack is possible, and put on general court and investigations. I sit on the only safe and possess the key. I'm becoming a postmaster at handling money from all over the world. I hope it balances out better than my checkbook did!"

Despite his own aggravation, Jim felt torn, as he didn't want to contribute to Ann's unhappiness as he felt that she was doing so much to support him. His family was constantly on his mind. His care and concern for them was unyielding as was his attention to his fellow soldiers. "Now I'm in a job that I'm not particularly qualified. I'll have to start scratching and quit worrying. Mr. Pooh regrets that all his letters aren't so sweet as to make you happy." He tried to ease her burden by making an effort to put a smile on her face with his cartoons and sense of humor.

When Jim got discouraged and was dogged with self-doubt, he wrestled with his decision to fight for people far away when he had a family who needed him at home. It reminded him of Mark Twain's Connecticut Yankee in King Arthurs's Court. In the book, a Yankee engineer from Connecticut receives a severe blow to the head and is somehow transported in time and space to England during the reign of King Arthur. He attempts to modernize the past in order to make people's lives better. Jim asked himself, *are my efforts in trying to make life better for those so far away worth the cost to my family?* He decided that, in the long run, his efforts would ultimately be beneficial to his family.

Although Jim felt that things were going well for the Allies, he didn't want to be overly optimistic, recalling that the last five yards to a touchdown are often the toughest. He reminded Ann to be patient. At the same time, he commented that the children were changing so much that he might not recognize them, especially Pie Pooh. "We'll have to get acquainted when I get home."

Many men, particularly fathers, serving in the war struggled with the conflict between serving their country and taking care of their families. Though the soldiers were getting paid and financially supporting those at home, they were absent from the daily lives of their loved ones. Most men were aware that their families had the additional burden of worrying about their soldier's safety.

While Jim was acting as chief fireman and police officer in response to the early morning plane crash during the Ploesti raid, Billy and Jimmy were enamored with the cops and firemen at a house fire in their neighborhood in Chevy Chase, MD. The Greene family casualties were Billy's broken leg and Jimmy's sprained knee. Their father suggested that it would be more worthwhile to buy bonds instead of paying doctor's bills. He congratulated them on selling war bonds and helping each other with their paper routes while they were recovering from their respective injuries.

Jim told his sons about the fine boys, just a little older than they were, who had become such good fighters. "Tall ones, short ones, fat ones, and skinny ones; those that like to play games and those that like to read. All of them go out and do their work well. They come back after a job like a bunch of kids let out of school, ready for a swim or a game and pack away great quantities of chow. They are modest and quiet about their exploits as if they had been shooting at sparrows with bb guns. It makes me feel good to know that you boys are the same sort of American boys who are polite and nice but who can fight so well and never boast about it."

A special treat for the boys was going to Glen Echo, a nine-acre amusement park near Washington, D.C. They loved riding the roller coaster, even with their mother along. The menagerie carousel was another favorite. It sported an operating brass ring. Daring riders could reach out and pull a ring out of a holder next to the carousel. Grabbing a brass ring would win the lucky rider a free ride. The competitive brothers would spend hours on the menagerie carousel, riding the 38 horses, two chariots, 4 rabbits, 4 ostriches, a lion, a tiger, a giraffe, and a prancing deer, and trying to capture the brass ring.

Periodically the boys would receive a memento from their father's desert scavenging. He sent them belt buckles, money from distant lands, replicas of plane markings, insignias, animal bones, and cartridges. The lack of rain preserved and sanitized everything. He assured them he would not send any annoying bedbugs. He looked forward to his sons' letters, but he told Ann, "Don't make the poor monkey tails write if they don't suggest it. I remember how I used to hate to write to people when I was a kid."

As their 13th anniversary approached on August 23rd, Jim relaxed under a few beautiful moonlit nights and reminisced of the moons he and Ann shared when they were "young and foolish." He sent her a cartoon to capture the memories. Since that eventful day, he joked that there was "just a little more water under the bridges." In other words, he teased that three children and a world war have barely impacted their lives or the world since they were married. Jim appreciated the virtues of his remarkable wife, though he thought she might have made a mistake choosing him. "You have done a far better missionary job on this old bear than anyone could have done."

Mentally returning to his present circumstances in Africa, Jim thought about his experiences in the Middle East and "determined that Americans work harder, play harder, and have more appreciation for the better things of life." He found them kinder and more thoughtful of others, though they could still stand a lot of improvement. "The people on top don't seem to have the vaguest idea that by helping the guys along the line you help yourself, even if the difference becomes less. It isn't accomplished with handouts. It starts with intelligent leadership, then better workmen, and last, better conditions. We have to sacrifice men to halt every war in the world before it starts and then let these people work out their own destiny."

Jim received a letter from Ed Walton at the advertising agency and thought about his homecoming. "Perhaps when I return, things will run along just as though I'd been off on a two-week vacation." He also thought how nice it would be to have someone help him with his correspondence as he preferred drawing to writing.

After the Sicily campaign, Jim settled down with the desert creatures for a nightly nap, looking forward to a break. He was due leave after serving for six months overseas but that was axed quickly because of his current responsibilities. He oversaw the honor guards for decoration ceremonies as the result of Ploesti and other missions, engaged in detective work for the British, and served on General Courts Martial for cases involving murder and misbehavior. The murder resulted in the end of two soldiers' careers. For a lesser offense, punishments might be more creative, like making a soldier dig a grave for stealing. When one of the men stole his dead tentmate's belongings, Jim made him dig the soldier's grave with his bare hands.

Notification was received that the Ninth Air Force was going to England. Rumors circulated within the 376th and 98th Groups regarding their possible departure from Africa. At the end of September, the speculation was put to rest when the Liberandos were ordered to a new base at Enfidaville, south of Tunis, in Tunisia. Enfidaville was liberated by French troops in April 1943. The 376th would become an element of the Twelfth Air Force under the command of Brigadier General James A. Doolittle. The move would bring the Group's B-

24s closer to strategic European targets as well as the tactical objectives in northern Italy.

The Liberandos had a few accomplishments and crucial experience to carry them into the next phase of the war. Endurance, fortitude, and courage were needed for the undetermined duration of the upcoming campaigns, beginning with attacks in southern Europe. Fighting for one's comrades was the biggest motivator.

Jim spent his last days at Berka 2 saying good-bye to his stray pets, sharing his cookies and water rations. He also said good-bye to Bob Storz, a pilot he flew with on one of the worst missions the Liberandos ever took. As a pilot, Bob could leave the combat area after a certain number of flights, usually about six months, while the ground crews and support forces were commissioned to stay much longer.

The new base was 1,200 miles from Berka 2. An advance party was sent a week ahead of the move to prepare the new base for the ground and air echelons. The ground crew convoy, comprised of 136 water and gas trucks, weapon and bomb carriers, ambulances, and jeeps, followed. Their mascot, a rickety fire truck confiscated from a previous base, served as caboose. The B-24s arrived last.

As the Liberandos prepared to travel across Africa, Jim became the Executive Officer of the 513th Squadron. He moved from the 514th Squadron with his expertise in intelligence, gunnery, and ground defense to lead the 513th Squadron. In addition, he was tasked with heading up the convoy of all four squadrons of the 376th Group on their eight-day trip to the new base.

The convoy pulled onto the Via Balbia, the only hard-surfaced road along the coast of North Africa, retracing Rommel's last retreat. The western route left the tree-shaded Benghazi surroundings and headed into the scrub desert and hills eroded into rocky spires and infinite other shapes. The first stop was near Agedabia, located on an arid plain 93 miles from Benghazi. The site is an important crossroads between the coastal road from Tripoli to Benghazi and inland routes south to the oasis at Jalu to Tobruk and the border with Egypt. Agedaia lies close to a large very hot dry region below sea level. British troops occupying the town readily provided their allies with gasoline for refueling the vehicles.

Finding adequate water sources was a major concern. Several wells contained bloated bodies of camels fouling the water and foreshadowed the difficulty and uncertainty of fulfilling their water needs. Such was the legacy of the Afrika Korps' last retreat.

At dusk the convoy camped on a stony plain with only an occasional thorn bush or shrub for shade. Signs in Arabic and English cautioned against investigating the Desert War wreckage littering the area. The retreating Germans had lingered long enough to set booby-traps, which might invite an explosion.

The next day's route followed the curved edge of the Gulf of Sirte. The terrain transitioned to salt marshes and sand dunes. Empty fuel drums dotted the sand covered road. Midday the convoy passed the remote outpost of El Agheila, a stucco fort atop a steep hill rising from the plain. During the Italian occupation of Libya, the town was the site of an Italian concentration camp for 10,000 nomadic Arabs, the Bedouins. Thousands of the Bedouins starved to death in the camp run by the Italian colonial troops.

In February 1941, El Agheila was taken by the British following their defeat of the Italians. The Germans had taken control of the area in March until Rommel was defeated at El Alamein. Finally, the Germans gave up control to the British in December 1942. A fluttering Union Jack announced its precarious British management.

The convoy replenished dwindling water and fuel supplies at a wayside inn called Casa Ristoro and drove through the imposing Marble Arch, an 80-foot edifice built by Mussolini in the 1930s during the early Italian occupation of Libya. It was situated on the dividing line between Tripolitania and Cyrenaica. Engraved on the spacious walls inside the arch were bas-reliefs heralding Mussolini's reign and extracts from his speeches. Near the arch's top were two bronze sculptures dedicated to the more deserving subjects, the Phileni brothers. The two Roman brothers were acclaimed athletes chosen to represent the empire in a boundary dispute. Ultimately, the brothers were accused of cheating during a physical contest to resolve the dispute. Legend says the arch is situated on the spot where the brothers were buried alive as punishment for their faulty character.

West of the Marble Arch, the country became a desert wasteland cut by dry washes or wadis. Bridges across the wadis were destroyed, necessitating long detours around them, often through soft sand or salt marshes. At one place steep escarpments on both sides of the wide dry riverbed required the use of ropes, chains and pulleys to negotiate the vehicles across the gorge. That evening the Liberandos made camp at a seaside oasis close to the Mediterranean Sea allowing for salt water baths. Malaria was an ever-present danger as the soldiers slept on cots in the open. Fortunately, no one was afflicted.

As the sun rose, the ensemble passed Sirte and crossed over the wide Wadi Tamet, and unknowingly went by a camouflaged German weather station, manned by English speaking Germans wearing British uniforms. The station continued to transmit to Axis headquarters on Crete until a suspicious Senussi native guided a British detachment to the location. As dusk descended, Jim was grateful for the safe progress the group was making.

A few trip annoyances occurred regularly along the route. When the convoy stopped for lunch, it had to stay on the road due to the danger of land mines. In addition, the sticky, crawling Egyptian flies would descend and fight for every morsel of food. Jim thought his little furry friends, like the stray dogs, rabbits, and hedgehogs, had much better manners.

Approaching the settlement of Misurata on a point overlooking the Mediterranean Sea, the bleak terrain became fertile and cultivated with thousands of date palms. The convoy made a brief halt to perform repairs on the deteriorating vehicles at the British Army garrison's motor pool. At noon on the fourth day, they reached the ancient Roman capital of Lepitus Magna, now known as Homs, with its well-preserved and imposing ruins and temples. The site had been a prewar mecca for archaeologists and was now surrounded by contrasting white buildings of modern architecture.

The convoy entered Tripoli on September 30th. Jim proclaimed a full day of rest for the tired and unkempt Liberandos. Several men seized the opportunity to explore the area, which had a place in U.S. history. From 1801-1805, Algiers, Tunis, and Tripoli were bases from which Barbary pirates preyed on ships in the Mediterranean Sea. During one of the new American nation's first engagements of war, the USS Philadelphia ran aground, was captured, and the entire crew taken prisoner. During captivity, they built Fort America.

Eventually, the USS Constitution recaptured the USS Philadelphia by hand-to-hand combat. The frigate couldn't be maneuvered to freedom so it was blown up.

The convoy resumed its journey in insufferable heat. The shade temperature of 136 degrees was recorded at El Azizia, a few miles south of Tripoli. Though Jim liked warm weather, it was hot!

A brief halt was made at another historically significant town, Sabratha, which dated to Phoenician times. Sabratha fell to the Romans and was a major trading port until the decline of the Roman occupation of North Africa.

West of Tripoli the true desert returned. The travelers passed through a wasteland devoid of human or animal life extending to the Tunisian border. Once in Tunisia, the coast road narrowed to little more than a trail frequently obscured by drifting sand. The pre-war French occupiers of Tunisia did not maintain a hard-surfaced road so as not to tempt an invasion from the opportunist Italians in Libya.

Approaching Gabes, the convoy passed through the massive fortifications of the Mareth line. The area was littered for miles with the material remains of the Afrika Korps' last battles in North Africa. The scattered litter had already been scavenged by the natives and what was left had no salvage or utility value. Gabes has a unique geographical feature in the world, featuring the mountains, the sea, the oasis and the desert. Camp for the night was made ten miles north of Gabes. Jim took a deep breath when he felt the salty air and smelled the sea. He was relieved and thankful the trip, so far, had been without incident after safely passing through the potential military danger zones and geographical challenges.

The convoy headed north along the coast to Sfax, an important seaport surrounded by a world-renowned olive grove. Sfax was a familiar target to the Liberandos. On December 16, 1942, nine of the 376th planes made the long trip from Egypt to drop 72 bombs on the shipping harbor with 69 scored hits. On the eve of their last day on the road, the weary Liberandos camped in a mine-free olive orchard 50 miles north of Sfax.

Proceeding north the next day, the convoy passed through Sousse, another settlement dating from the Roman era. The city was featured in the Third Sicilian War, the Second and Third Punic Wars and Caesar's Civil War. Its native sons included the jurist Salvius Julianus, the emperor Clodius Albinus and numerous Christian saints. The Roman and Byzantine catacombs beneath the city are extensive. The waterfront district, like Sfax, showed the scars left from two 1942 raids by the 376th Liberandos. Visible in the harbor were the hulks of several ships. As a student of history, Jim was saddened by the damage done. It reinforced the importance of target accuracy, and he spent the rest of the war emphasizing it.

North of Sousse, where the final energy of the Afrika Korps was expended, the land took on the climate, soil and fertility of southern California. The green tones of the cultivated areas were a welcome relief to eyes nearly blinded by the daily glare of desert sand. The countryside was a maze of hills and valleys cut by numerous wadis. A network of dirt roads connected obscure towns.

Some 60 miles south of Tunis, the convoy left the coast road and pulled into the 376th's new home, an abandoned German airfield within sight of Enfidaville. A vast plain extended to the east and south of the new airfield. North and west, bare eroded hills rose to rounded and flat-topped summits. Less than an hour west, Tunisia's highest peak reached 5,000 feet into the clouds. The hills radiated color tones varying from blue, yellow, purple and chocolate brown, depending on the time of day. This citadel had been wrested from the Germans by the French Nineteenth Corps only a few months before.

The majestic beauty and calm of the environs allowed Jim and his comrades a safe respite from their exhausting trip. He was humbled by the awesome surroundings and grateful to be given the opportunity to see this part of the world. He was so appreciative of the men and their successful completion of the long journey. After a brief interlude, Jim was back to setting up living quarters and organizing the next mission.

Tent accommodations were the same as in previous camps with one improvement. Kairouan, the manufacturing center for hand-made rugs and carpets, lay several miles south. These works of art were woven from undyed wool of the multi-colored desert sheep. Liberandos purchased them to cover the dirt floors of their tents.

Outbreaks of illnesses were minimized due to sanitation adjustments made from experiences of previous desert bases. However, flies were more prevalent and a lack of adequate screening caused numerous cases of diarrhea. The improved food was a worthy exchange for the loss of the Benghazi seashore. Once the base was established, the Liberando School resumed and taught languages, public speaking, and other courses for off-duty activities.

The experiences of Jim's tentmates highlighted the dangers of his current environment. "I'm living alone because my tent-mate, Captain J.W. Ewen, went to the hospital with a broken collar bone and possibly a rib. Whenever that happens you never see them again; at least that is my observation. People are sort of like equipment. When you can't fix it, you leave it, and the next outfit gets it. You salvage whatever you find with due respect to the booby traps. Every captain I've lived with has wound up in the hospital. It seems if I get chummy with someone then he gets cracked up or shot down. I'm going to start playing the field before I get the reputation of being a jinx."

One afternoon Jim observed a severely injured child being brought to the squadron for medical attention. He shared his thoughts with Ann. "The people were very stoical when bringing wounded children on donkeys. The injured would rate an ambulance at home."

This reflection reminded Jim of all Ann did for him and the family. "Who protects me from little bears when I have my nose in the radio? Who is the heroine when the little bears get smashed up or squeal in the middle of the night? Who keeps the checkbook straight and pays all the bills with half the money necessary? Who never has all the nice things her friends with smarter husbands have? Who has the best home and the happiest family of all? And then she makes people believe that the fat old lazy daddy bear does the work. He just basks in reflected glory and absorbs the wonderful plaudits for the job his wife does."

Jim inspected some graves before the engineers put barbed wire around them. Most soldiers were buried right where they fell so there were seldom more than a dozen graves at a site. Several men were buried in double graves; two brothers were buried together. Visiting the graves, Jim realized how fortunate he was not to be in the Infantry.

Jim received word that his best friend, Sam Syme, who was serving with Patton, was in the hospital. "I passed several field hospitals not long ago and would have checked all of them, though finding someone is like looking for a needle in a haystack. Military secrecy and the movement of patients would have made it difficult for me to find him." Sam meant the world to him and Jim hoped Sam was getting the medical care that he needed. Again, Jim was reminded of the fragility of life and how devastating war was to so many.

During the last days of August and the first half of September 1943, many of the Liberando crews accumulated the required 300 combat hours and finished their tours. They had come through the fury of numerous air battles which had taken the lives of many comrades since training days. Some had survived being shot down, illness, and hospital recuperation.

Their departure prompted a flurry of replacements. The new crew got a taste of combat with simulated attacks at the base as part of their indoctrination.

Missions to southern Europe resumed shortly after setting up at Enfidaville. The 376th tactical bombing supported British operations in the Greek Dodecanese Islands in the Aegean Sea off the coast of Turkey. Enemy aircraft based in Greece and Crete harassed ships and convoys supporting Allied beachheads. American-controlled harbors on the Italian mainland were attacked daily.

The versatile Liberandos knocked out numerous Italian bridges and viaducts, many spanning deep gorges over streams and major rivers. These major thoroughfares were essential to the German transportation system. Low level surprise attacks similar to the Ploesti attack and earlier raids on the Sicilian ferry terminals were successful as the BBC proclaimed, "Ploesti Raiders Strike Again!"

Ball bearings were a critical component in tanks, airplanes, and any mechanical piece of equipment. The Liberandos briefly focused their attention on ball bearing manufacturing plants, particularly near Turin, Italy. The 376th made several attacks on these targets without much success that fall.

On October 29th, the Liberandos took a moment to welcome Major General James Doolittle for an awards ceremony. All of the men wanted to look sharp and professional for the presentation. In the absence of a laundry service, they touched up their uniforms with a somewhat dangerous improvised cleaning fluid: 100% octane gas. Maintaining a shine on shoes while treading over a dusty field was a challenge. Jim presented the Ploesti Raiders for decoration. Some of the low-level Ploesti pilots received Distinguished Flying crosses.

The conclusion of the North African campaign and the success of the Italian invasion led to a two-front strategic air offensive against Germany from England and Italy. However, Hitler signed a formal order demanding the end of withdrawals in Italy. The Allies underestimated German resolve in thinking Hitler would abandon southern Italy. As a result, the Liberandos were sorely needed in that arena. General Doolittle, the new leader of the Fifteenth Air Force division, announced that the 376th would be part of the 47th Wing of this division and relocate to Italy. The Fifteenth remained a vital component until the end of the war.

The end of the month brought a pay-day surprise and the Red Cross. The soldiers were given their pay in American gold-seal dollars and silver currency.

This was unusual because normally they were paid with nondescript dollars and coins. Many payees went directly to the post office to have money orders sent home rather than being enticed into a card game. Others were able to avoid local temptations as the money had sentimental value and they didn't want to part with it. The American Red Cross opened a well-received men's club providing hospitality, food and recreation.

Jim had time to send some fatherly advice to his sons:

"Jim, congratulations on being the president of your class. Think about what you can do to make it the best class in the school. That means you won't have time to think about yourself except to be sure to do everything right so as to be an example for others.

"Bill, it is nice to hear you have a new wristwatch. Watches and clocks are very scarce over here. Both of mine are out of commission. You can get some desert sand out of my watches when I get home.

"I'm enclosing our squadron insignia. The men sew them on the left side of their leather jackets over their hearts and wear them like a football letter. They are very proud of them. Another symbol is a diamond. All our tents and junk are marked with a diamond so nobody will swipe them.

"We got the World Series 'inning by inning' score by radio. Sorry Washington, D.C. didn't win the pennant but second place isn't bad. I reckon you are enjoying the football season. I sure will be glad when I get back and can go to the games with you.

Love,
Daddy"

Mid-November, just as the Liberandos were getting used to their new base, they were assigned to another location at San Pancrazio, Italy. As they prepared to leave, Jim thought about the bomber, The *Lady Be Good*, lost on one of the Naples missions on April 4th. The crew still had not been located. Jim was haunted by its disappearance, especially as he was part of the investigation team. It was extremely rare not to know the whereabouts of planes that failed to return to base. In addition, on an unusual flight for him, he had flown in the plane directly in front of the *Lady Be Good*. He was prohibited from flying on missions in his capacity and could have been discharged from the Air Corps. Now, he would be leaving North Africa without solving this mystery. He would think about the fate of the plane often in the years to come.

Before Jim left Africa, he sent several letters, handmade cards, and packages in celebration of Thanksgiving, Ann's and Bill's December birthdays, and Christmas. He anticipated mail delays and could not foresee the unknown in Italy.

These sure are powerfull field glasses Uncle Sam gives his old captains

"One birthday card for two; that's war economy. When Bill was one year old, Mamu was 30 times as old as he was. Now he's ten, Mother is only four times as old, so Bill is getting older and Mamu is getting younger. Many happy returns.

"The other day I looked over a nearby town (Tunis) and saw the most civilized people by our standards. The area was not as badly wrecked as most places. I got a haircut, an omelet, two leather donuts, and something called coffee. It was my first civilized food in seven months. I saw white ladies pushing baby buggies and walking children and a few civilian autos passed me. The sight actually made me feel homesick. We headed back to camp to the usual GI rolling stock. I've gotten so accustomed to it. I almost forgot any other kind of world existed.

"…I get paid 10% overseas on base pay, which is about $90 after the deductions of your allotment, my insurance, and the month's rations at 70 cents a day. I can send home about $150 every two months after I buy a few necessities. (Jim kept $15 a month.) Two eggs cost 20 cents when we can get them. The liquor is local stuff. The laundry is several bucks each time.

"It has turned quite cold, especially at night. We have an oil-stove in the tent and plenty of blankets. It's not bad until I have to get up and go outside. I've actually gotten so I wake up before dawn even on the days I could sleep. Normal breakfast time is when I get hungry for lunch. I'll have to revolutionize my habits when I get home."

"…I feel the same loneliness you do… I think of the great day when the war is won. Private, captain, or general, WACC, or housewife, we have a clear conscience and know we finished it."

The planning and execution of the next move was fraught with complications and tragedy. Key ground crews loaded into Liberators flew to the new location. A thunderstorm separated the planes and one of the bombers crashed into the sea, resulting in loss of personnel and military records. Several planes were damaged in landing. Most personnel, the heavy equipment, trucks, jeeps, ambulances, tents, etc. followed by ship. Eventually, the Liberandos arrived in San Pancrazio, Italy. This location was to be their home base for the duration of the war in the European Theatre.

The Liberandos shook the dust of Africa from their feet. The soldiers didn't miss the days of relentless heat and nights of bitter cold or the dust storms, mice and rats. They were especially relieved to say good-bye to the dangerous scorpions. From their new base, the mature and seasoned 376th Bombardment Group was prepared to continue the fight. Many achievements gave them confidence to meet the coming days with courage tempered by sadness.

Chapter 9
A Difficult Loss

Jim traveled by ship to "San Pan," an existing airfield located between the Gulf of Taranto on the west side of the heel of Italy and Brindisi to the east on the Adriatic Sea. He rode through a few villages on his way from the harbor to the new base. All local able-bodied men were in the Italian service so the women, children and old men were left to fend for themselves the best they could. The children were a bit skinny. Most of the towns looked pretty poverty stricken and seemed happy to see the U.S. servicemen. "Once Uncle Sam steps in, nobody starves." The United States provided much needed food to the Italian prisoners and civilians.

The Liberandos' relocation was complicated by constant rain. Twenty-three inches fell in the last three months of 1943. The first weeks were a struggle for survival in a sea of mud with swarming rats. The 376th repaired and waterproofed tents before the winter cold arrived. Roads were sorted out, drainage ditches were dug, garbage was cleaned up, and strict sanitation was enforced. Fortunately, Jim had better accommodations due to the deluge.

"I'm living comfortably in spite of constant rain, which is causing my tent to be in a mud hole. Several of us are sleeping in a nearby barn with a fireplace. We look out at our tent now and then to be sure it hasn't blown away. I walk about two miles to the shower. The first shower I have taken in a long time. It is very nice to be in a civilized country with a few trees and plenty of grass. We do miss the glamour of the sheiks and harems in Africa. Some of our fiction writers have vivid imaginations.

"We have a 15-year-old French refugee taking care of us. I saw some Itie women doing wash so I gave them mine. The people are very friendly as are the Italian soldiers. Quite a few people speak French so I can make myself understood.

"Let's think about Thanksgiving. The Poohs really have lots to be thankful for in addition to being free white Americans. We are all healthy, which is most important. We aren't faced with any kind of want. When the war is over, the Poohs will be reunited.

"That's as close to heaven as mere bears can get in this world.

"My candle has given out so I must write by flashlight, which is difficult."

During November and December, San Pan was one of more than 45 airfields in Italy being prepared for combat. The Allied takeover of these airfields gave them control of the Italian skies. Engineers laid an aviation gas pipeline providing 160,000 gallons of fuel each week to the Fifteenth Air Force bases. The Adriatic Depot was established at Bari to handle American Air Force supplies. The largest network of wire communications to date was built. Permanent first-class construction of wire lines, cable routes, test points and airfield distribution systems required blasting through stone strata to bury and protect them from disruption.

Jim benefited from this work because he was able to receive and share valuable information from a much larger geographic area. Better planning decisions could be made with consistent, accurate information from multiple sources, saving untold lives and preserving hundreds of aircraft. For example, VHF radio, using the call sign BIG FENCE, was the "Big Friend" of airmen in Africa and Italy. It was particularly useful to fighter aircraft with their limited radio and navigation gear. VHF radio also seemed like a heavenly angel to the aircraft in distress or to the bomber contemplating an emergency landing at sea. BIG FENCE handled a record number of 108 calls in one day and over 16,000 during the wartime operation.

In spite of horrendous conditions, one week after arriving in Italy, the 376th flew its first mission from San Pan to the marshalling yards at Sofia, Bulgaria. The bomb routes were much longer as the geographic area expanded, sending crews through varying weather patterns. Temperatures ranged from furnace heat to arctic cold at higher altitudes. Extra oxygen masks were necessary when masks froze up.

Two weeks after the Liberandos' arrival on December 2, 1943, the German Air Force made the most devastating bombing attack since the Japanese attack on Pearl Harbor. Seventeen Allied ships with sorely needed cargo were destroyed in Bari Harbor on the east coast of Italy. At least 1,000 people were killed or missing, and many records were lost during this attack.

Over 600 injuries were caused by chemical mustard exposure. The mustard bombs were secretly shipped to Bari because President Roosevelt had become alarmed by reports that the Axis might use chemical agents. He issued a statement declaring that Americans would not use poisonous or noxious gases unless they were used by the enemy first. The Bari bombing was a serious setback to combat operations in Italy. However, the 376th was back to work the next day.

December was one of the saddest months of the war for the Liberandos. After four missions, 13 bombers were lost in combat, two were lost in landing crashes, and many more were heavily damaged. One hundred thirty crewmen were missing in action and many more injured. As a result, the 376th was taken off combat operations to undergo an almost complete personnel turnover. The pilots and their accompanying flight crews who had served in the Middle East and North Africa, and had completed their required missions went back to the States.

While Jim was getting settled in Italy, the Greene family was preparing for the holidays. A friend thought publishing a family picture in the newspaper acknowledging a father off at war would capture this period in time. Ann obliged and a Washington Post photographer captured the Greene family in a scene familiar in many homes that Christmas. The caption read, "It's Mama this year who has to put the electric train together, and carry on for the whole family. In this case it is Mrs. James Frances Greene, wife of Captain Greene, U.S. Army. Jimmy, Jr., Billy and Ann, who packed Daddy's Christmas stocking in time for it to reach him overseas before the holidays and for him to send word of its safe arrival; inspect their own stockings and help Mama with that job on the electric train." A photograph of their father was placed on the mantle overseeing the activity.

Ann and the children sent Daddy's gifts in time to reach him before Christmas. Jim's stocking contained Hershey bars and cigarettes and included the following poem, with apologies to Walt Whitman:

O Captain! My Captain our
fearful fever's done.
Mrs. Pooh has weathered every job
our freedom now is won.
The boys are at school, where bells do
rule, and I am all exulting!
While cleaning house with Ann at
heel, or all around me tearing.
But o joy, joy, joy,
the welcome postman's ring.
For letters from my Captain
at last for me he did bring.

O Captain, my Captain to hear
and know you are well
To know for you a rest was had,
now comfort where you dwell.
For you a decoration, for you
a ribbon blue.
But for me a gingham apron
And a dishpan's greasy hue
But Captain! dear Father!
I'll still hold high my head!
Even tho' my dream of major
Has fallen cold and dead!

My Captain, we're still proud of you
Cubs and I are waiting here.
My captain does not feel my arms
Tho' I know he'd like 'em near!

When the war is won all safe
and sound, its purpose closed and done.
Turn fearful trip the captain
comes in with object won.
We'll wave our flags and wave our bells
And I with quickened tread
will greet the plane my Captain flies
And then who'll earn the bread?

Winter arrived mid-January in Washington, D.C. with sleet, hail, and an afternoon snow that lasted through the night. The children made snowballs and played on the sled. They enjoyed a fun break from the usual school routine. Extracurricular activities continued, if somewhat limited by the war and the absence of adult volunteers. Jimmy was looking forward to moving up from Cub Scouts to Boy Scouts as soon as there was a vacancy, but spaces were limited due to a lack of troop leaders.

Little Ann remembered her train trip last winter and begged her mother to take her on another trip to see her daddy. During a shopping outing, Ann announced to the store in a loud voice, "My daddy's fighting for that 'merican flag," much to the delight and amazement of clerks and customers. Her enthusiasm would have been welcomed in Italy.

Jim's new year began on a very sad note. Ann sent a telegram with devastating news on January 2nd. Jim's best childhood friend, Sam, had died of pneumonia while serving on General Patton's staff in Algiers. Sam's only sibling was serving far away in the Aleutians, Alaska. His mother, wife, and nine-year-old son survived him. He was a well-known lawyer and professor in Washington, D.C. and his death was a shock to the entire community. Ann's fears for Jim were exacerbated with the death of their dear friend. "I find myself worrying more and more about my old man's health and wellbeing. Do please take care of yourself and come home safe and sound. This is my prayer every waking minute of my waking hours."

Jim thought about losing his best friend and, having winked back tears, responded, "The idea of being shocked by death over here now really doesn't exist in the sense of normal times over there. When I come home, I think the shocks will hit me. Georgetown will be without the expected older folks and have many who have lost husbands and brothers and sons. I'll have to guard against hurting people. I won't have the friends to share experiences. It will be worse not having those who won't be where they should be than picking up what is left of somebody you knew for a short time, or never hearing from them again. You pick up the personal effects, wonder for a day. The replacements come and you move on." Jim cared for his comrades and did his best to protect them from danger, but he was realistic about the human cost of war. He was coming to terms with the changed complexion of his community on his return to Washington D.C., he would have to be compassionate and not boast of the Liberandos' accomplishments.

As crew replacements arrived daily in sparkling bright aluminum Liberators, Jim spent many hours getting to know the new recruits in the squadron. He reminded them that even though they were far from home, they fought so that this war would not reach United States shores and fellow Americans would continue to enjoy the freedoms they had come to know. As the personnel changed so did the older model pink and drab green B-24s flown in the Mediterranean Theatre. The pilots and crews concentrated on new formation flying, practice bombing, and special training programs. Preparations for OVERLORD (D-Day) and a simultaneous attack in Provence, France, were underway. It was later decided to postpone the southern France attack. None of the operations would be successful unless the German Air Force was significantly curtailed.

By mid-February, the 376th had 58 B-24s and 65 combat crews. They aspired not only to finish a creditable tour of duty but also to attain the coveted status of a lead crew. A pilot usually could expect to fly with an experienced crew three or four times before being scheduled to fly with his own crew. Flight crews were subjected to long strenuous days in combat, flying three consecutive missions before taking a mission off for rest, training, and other duties.

The maintenance crew played an integral part in keeping missions on schedule. Weather, the great enemy of the flying man, was the chief challenge of the maintenance man as well. Southern Italy in mid-winter saw mud, rain, sleet, and a stepped-up tempo of operations. The men kept the ships flying in the freezing darkness. Since they couldn't do the intricate work necessary while wearing gloves, their hands chafed raw by icy, high-test gasoline.

Ingenuity created a few conveniences for tent living in the winter months. Discarded materials were used to make showers and heaters. A disposable wing gas tank from a fighter plane and a sprinkler made a much-used shower, a real treasure. Cast-off oil drums became gasoline burning stoves. Gasoline ran through improvised external tanks and salvaged aircraft valves and tubing. Unfortunately, fires from misbehaving stoves resulted in serious damage to tents and a few serious burns caused at least one death. Jim described some of his makeshift amenities. "We have an oil stove in the tent and plenty of blankets. Since it is cold as blue blazes, everyone has given up on washing."

On the war front, the cold overcast winter months magnified the lack of acknowledgement of the 376th accomplishments by the press. Pilots and crews, squadrons and groups competed like sports teams and when they won, they wanted credit. Jim shared his momentary frustration of his U. S. Air Force Group being outshined by a British Air Force Group. According to him, the press was providing inaccurate information.

"That publicity stuff is a funny thing. We're beginning to get a little now and it sounds silly. The people in the Eighth Air Force (Britain) really think they have a tougher time than the Fifteenth Air Force. Statistics prove things are equal but we're in a much less attractive and congenial place and aren't as big (of an outfit.) We (the United States) don't give half the decorations that they do because our policy is not to cheapen the Distinguished Flying Cross. Yank magazine actually ran a feature story on shuttle runs to Russia showing pictures of our men and crediting the Eighth. Engine advertisers in magazines talk about the Eighth and never mention us. I suppose, even if they had the facts, they wouldn't mention us because the public wouldn't understand. A 376th corporal just sighs as he thinks of his five service stripes and nine battle stars."

Jim's attitude brightened as the weather improved and the Liberandos were recognized. A few highlights of the winter months came in February. Seventeen German aircraft were destroyed and six planes were damaged at the Viterbo Airdrome near Rome, Italy. The 376th sent 24 aircraft for the successful attack of the Obertraubling assembly plant. Thirty-three B-24s successfully attacked the Steyrwaffen Walzlagerwerk ballbearing factory in Steyr, Austria.

On March 4, 1944, General Nathan F. Twining presented a Presidential Citation to the Liberandos for their continuous and sustained operations against the enemy in strategic support of the Allied Forces in the Middle East and North African Theatres of war from June 2, 1942 to December 1943. The completion of its 200th mission symbolized the aggressiveness with which the group operated from the outset of combat operations. Twining's address highlighted their efforts, "The exemplary devotion to duty and the high efficiency shown by both flying and ground personnel, in flying and maintaining the aircraft of the Group despite the desert hardships, extremely difficult problems of logistics, inferior rations, and the lack of sufficient men and material under severe battle conditions is worthy of the highest commendation."

Assaults against Balkan targets began in April in direct support of the Russian armies. Prime targets were the rail lines the Germans needed to supply their troops in Rumania and southern Russia. The most vital communication centers were Bucharest, Ploesti, Sofia, and Budapest. In Bucharest, approximately 1,600 rail cars were destroyed, along with repair shops, military barracks, a chemical factory, oil refineries and oil storage and ammunition dumps. It took months for the Germans to patch the rail lines and yards. Finally, the Rumanian Air Force was broken. The Bucharest mission on May 7th was the 250th for the 376th. Colonel Hugo Rush presented special medals to 19 officers and enlisted men. His closing words, "This 250th mission against the enemy is a tribute to the ground crews who have kept the planes flying."

Spring also lifted the spirits of those in Washington, D.C. The weather was milder, and the roses were blooming. Ann took a bouquet from her garden when she visited Admiral Leahy in the hospital. The neighborhood Victory Gardens were planted and both boys helped keep the weeds out. Jim and Bill built a rabbit house and yard for the Easter bunny that they gave their little sister, Ann. One day climaxed with a trip to Walter Reed Hospital to have Jimmy's knee sewed up as the result of an ugly bike wreck. The boys bought a corsage for their mother for Mother's Day, and sent Jim a Father's Day card, reminding him how much he was missed and loved.

Ann tried to manage a household without any money from Jim since January. As always, she was concerned about the financial picture. Jim told her to expect an extra $75 a month after deductions for his insurance and rations. He paid $21 a month for his meals and saved $15 for spending money. At this point, she depended so much on Jim's letters to lift her morale.

The Greene family did major spring cleaning in anticipation of visitors. Ann especially enjoyed a surprise visit from cousin, Albert Rhett Stuart, who was headed out of the country as a United States Naval Reserve chaplain. After the war he had a distinguished career when he later became the Episcopal Bishop of Georgia, a civil rights advocate, and a friend of Martin Luther King, Jr. Family visits and gatherings continued with those still in town. Holidays and birthdays brought young and old together. Relatives and friends passing through Washington, D.C. made it a point to visit in order to share the latest information of those dear ones dispersed around the globe. Oftentimes, those who had died or fallen in combat were remembered. General Marshall and Admiral Leahy attended when in town, although the latest gathering had to be postponed due to the admiral's hospital stay prompted by a bout with pneumonia.

Jim was finally promoted to Major after carrying out the responsibilities of that rank for quite a while. Family and friends celebrated from afar. The news spread quickly and congratulations were expressed all around. Young Jim was very proud of his father but wished Jim was available to attend the father-son outing and play in the ball game with him. "Gee, I wish Dad were here. He could really show them how to play!"

Instead of participating in a baseball game, Jim helped plan the next missions. In particular, he helped decide the personnel involved and the targets to attack. Colonel Rush instituted a new offensive flying formation for the 376th. He preferred three divisions of 12 planes instead of two groups of 18 per section. The AAF Board in Orlando completed comprehensive tests. The pilots found the 12-plane formation easier to fly and more maneuverable with a superior defensive capability.

The Fifteenth Air Force, of which the 376th was part, had tripled in strength and reached maturity. In early May, the Fifteenth dropped a greater bomb load surpassing the Eighth, which had twice its capacity. Bombing accuracy was now being measured, recorded and published for each group. The accuracy of bombs was measured by the percentage of bombs within 1,000 feet of the target. The 47th Wing, including the 376th, achieved an accuracy of 52% and took first place with the 376th leading the divisions.

After two months of attacks on transportation routes, Operation STRANGLE cut the daily supplies to the enemy in Italy from 4,000 tons to 1,500 tons. The enemy lacked food, clothing, munitions, fuel, and transport. Some German tanks with empty gas tanks were being towed by oxen. At this point, the 376th reached a record 75% bombing accuracy.

At the end of May, the Fifteenth struck the 14 most important rail centers in southern France with 3,200 tons of high explosives. The bombing set a new record with 100% of the bombs hitting within 2,000 feet of the aiming point and 60% within 1,000 feet. Next, 530 bombers blasted the Wiener Neustadt target complex in Austria and 126 B-24s struck and destroyed the main ME-109 component factory buildings at Atzgersdorf, Austria, making German manufacturing impossible.

The Bratislava, Czechoslovakia mission on June 16, 1944 earned the 376th its third Presidential Unit Citation. The 376th was the only Bomb Group receiving such an award for a single mission. Approximately 90% of the bombs were dropped within 1,000 feet of the target.

The usual time for a crew to complete a combat tour of 50 missions, eventually reduced to 35 missions, was about four months. One crew member finished in a record 77 days, but many others weren't able to complete their missions. Planes were shot down resulting in injury, death, or capture. Few crews completed their 50 missions as a unit with all of their original members. Combat casualties, illness, and special duty assignments were a few of the reasons a crew's integrity was broken. When an airman completed his tour, the flight surgeon examined and certified his rotation eligibility to go back to the U.S. Processing to the States was rapid. Re-assignment included non-combat tasks around the globe or training to return to combat. Pilots, bombardiers, and navigators were the airmen who returned home after they flew their required number of missions. The ground crews usually stayed for the duration.

Jim was part of the ground crew. He had been gone from home almost two years, one year stateside and one year abroad. He didn't enjoy administrative work; he preferred actual combat as part of a flight crew. However, Jim respected military authority and knew that giving his all to each task was his best contribution to the war effort.

Life was not all fighting. A sightseeing tour of a few historical places in Italy, spared from bombs, gave him a change that helped energize him for the next phase of the war. He regained his positive attitude and carried on.

Chapter 10
Moseying Around

After serving over a year in the Middle East Theatre, Jim took advantage of a few days off to visit Rome, Bari, Naples, and Vesuvius. One day, he toured St. Peter's Basilica with a captain and a lieutenant and had an experience to share. The men were in a wing of the building looking at paintings by some of the Old Masters when they heard a racket at a side door and went to investigate. They found a crowd of people walking up a big stairway toward them. A guard leading the group said that the visitors were waiting for an audience with the Pope.

The three officers fell in at the head of the crowd and were ushered into a chapel about the size of the Bethlehem Chapel at the National Cathedral. Papal Guards handed out little medallions blessed by the Pope. They seated Jim and his fellow soldiers on a dais at the foot of the Pope's throne.

When the church was filled, the guards assigned to the pope, dressed in blue and yellow striped suits, wearing helmets, and carrying halberds and spears, marched in. Behind them came Pope Pius XII, "the old boy sitting in a houdah," borne on the shoulders of members of the guard. When he got to where they were, he climbed onto his throne and gave a speech in English, French, and Italian. He welcomed them to Vatican City and hoped the war would be over soon so the soldiers could return to their families. Following the speech, he blessed them and came down so everyone could kiss his ring.

Jim's comment on his adventure, "It was a good show. I have to hand it to the old boy.

"He has an excellent personality and a lot of character in his face. Undoubtedly, he is a swell gent. I reckon that about winds up the famous people I'll see until I meet God. I hope it won't be soon. Beginning with General Pershing, and trifling along with Lady Astor, Admiral Leahy, General

Alexander, General Marshall, the King of Greece, and finally the Pope. Five kings, three commanding generals and all the other celebrities is quite a lot for one small Pooh Bear."

Upon his return to San Pan, Jim helped create a recuperative environment to boost morale. Support personnel labored around the clock to keep the aircraft operating in hot and humid Italy and appreciated an occasional respite from the base. A private beach a few miles from San Pan on the Gulf of Taranto, equipped with a raft for diving and lounging, was a cherished destination. The beach became a favorite spot for Jim to swim some laps when he could steal a few hours away from his responsibilities.

While Jim was spending his summer in Italy, Jimmy took his father's footlocker and boarded the train to upstate New York for an adventure at Camp Red Cloud. The camp was located near Plattsburgh, where his father had attended combat training for World War I in 1918. Jimmy learned to row, played water polo and baseball, rode horses, became proficient in riflery, and took a course in junior lifesaving. A funny evening activity was a soccer match between the counselors. The men wore dresses and the women, from neighboring Camp Red Wing, wore men's clothes. In addition to camp activities, the campers attended church and heard a talk on friendship and how to help "the other fellow." Jimmy commented that he occasionally was homesick, but he got over it.

Ann continued the family correspondence with her 200th letter to Jim. She shared that she delivered the newspapers after Bill was stung by a bee.

Fortunately, he recovered in time to participate in the county playgrounds track meet, winning three first places.

Ann was happy to hear good news from all war fronts. She finally learned where Jim was stationed through the winter and spring during a visit from his brother, Walter Peter. She didn't know exactly where he was, based on his letters, due to safety precautions. Walter heard the confidential information from a family friend. She was somewhat relieved to know that he was at a distance from the ground war.

Ann commented on the election, "Dad seems to be weathering the heat and the 'election mudslinging.'" Her father, Edgar Smith, was an avid supporter of President Roosevelt, who was seeking an unprecedented fourth term. This would be the last time in which an incumbent Democratic president would win re-election after serving a full term in office until 1996. Though Roosevelt won the election, he only served three months and died before the end of the war. Vice President Harry S. Truman became the next president.

On the European front, July wasn't kind to the Liberandos. The 376th lost 12 B-24s with 120 crew members. Fifteen out of 20 missions returned with wounded men aboard and either major or minor aircraft damage. Whenever a returning plane was in trouble with battle damage and/or injured crew members, the air base emergency system was alerted by radio and red flares. Firefighters and medical people raced to the stricken aircraft. Jim managed the casualties of these missions by notifying family of the deceased, planning funerals, sending personal items home, and making arrangements for wounded soldiers.

On a positive note, *Flame McGoon*, a B-24 bomber of the 513th squadron flew its 75th consecutive mission without a turnback due to mechanical failure. This aircraft joined the 376th in Enfidaville, flying many rough missions from the desert before moving to San Pan. *Flame McGoon's* unequalled record, perhaps Air Force wide, was a credit to its dedicated maintenance crew. For example, the bomber returned from one attack with wing tanks riddled with bullet holes. With no replacement parts available, the crew installed a bomb bay tank in the sleeting darkness and presented the plane for the next day's mission. Five nights in a row, the bomb bay tank was removed or replaced as the ship flew alternate long and short missions. On another attack, the bomber returned so badly mangled that one wing, an elevator, two super-chargers, the right rudder and the wing flaps had to be replaced. The electrical system and hydraulic lines were shot out. The leading edge of the remaining wing was riddled and the right tire was flat. To the amazement of the sweating mechanics, all ten of the flying crew stepped out unscathed. During *Flame McGoon's* eventful career, no crewmember was killed.

Finally, on its 76th and last mission, it received a direct hit and was engulfed in flames. Before the plane crashed near Bor, Yugoslavia, the pilot and crew bailed out and became POWs. Jim was constantly amazed at the dedication and creativity of the men with whom he worked.

The Fifteenth concluded its twenty 1944 Ploesti raids with a four-wing attack on August 18th and a single wing attack on August 19th. The enemy launched no aircraft to intercept this Ploesti mission. Ploesti flak, however, exacted its last toll, destroying two B-17s. The Germans fought on, however, until August 30th when Ploesti was captured. Eight days later Rumania surrendered to the Russians. It was followed by the fall of Bucharest on August 31st. The Soviets now held one third of Rumania. Generals Ira C. Eaker and Twining determined that due to the continuously sustained effort, the attacks destroyed the enemy's oil production. General Twining stated, "The Ploesti Air Battle was the climax of one of strategic air power's greatest triumphs, a five-month campaign carried out by bombers and fighters of the Mediterranean Strategic Air Force based in Italy. The overall effect of Ploesti's loss to the enemy is becoming more noticeable every day – on the battlefields of Europe where a battered Wehrmacht is fast losing its mobility; in the air where the Luftwaffe is virtually grounded; in the core of German industrial economy – all for lack of gas alone and oil so vital in the now hopeless fight against the ring of steel closing ever tighter around the heart of Germany."

The cost of this conquest was high, with the 376th recording 152 killed or missing Liberandos as well as 19 lost and 15 severely damaged aircraft. The Liberandos saw the equivalent of almost one complete squadron's aircraft and crews wiped out in each of the past two months.

Jim and other executives had to address a major problem of limited manpower and its effect on morale due to the heavy losses. The rotation policy was very important to the morale of the combat crewman. A combat commander had upbeat crews when there were two crews per aircraft eagerly seeking combat time to complete their tour. Now there was only one crew per bomber.

In addition, some combat crewmen didn't want to fly. As a crewman neared the end of his combat mission requirement, his worries increased. Fear of flying is present in peacetime and compounded in combat. Approximately 40% of returning combat crewmen stated that they were afraid almost every time they flew and another 44% said they were afraid 75% of the time. About 33% considered asking to be grounded while 4% actually quit. At this juncture, Jim spent a great deal of time encouraging the men in his squadron to complete their missions. He allowed them to express their concerns and shared the success rates of the pilots of the crews and the planes in which they would be flying.

Ann's noticeable loss of weight due to the stress of the war was evident in a photograph she sent to Jim. She sought medical care and on a return visit to her doctor, she addressed pregnancy prevention. In anticipation of Jim's return, she asked him to "fix her up so she wouldn't have to worry over future bambinos when you return." As was common at the time, her doctor reminded Ann that she would have to have Jim's consent in writing before he could proceed. Ann asked Jim to write a letter to Dr. Boyd giving his consent. She explained to Jim that the procedure was a minor operation and would require a few days in the hospital. She added that it would relieve her of worries as she has "all the bambinos I can afford, financially, physically, or emotionally. However, if you feel otherwise, skip it." Jim supported her without question.

There were a number of household expenses that challenged Ann's ingenuity. She lamented that she had to ask the ration board for extra shoe stamps. She even used some of her father's stamps to keep their growing children in shoes. Bill's drum had to be mended after Ann punched a hole in it. This was a necessary expense as he had to have a working drum for band when school resumed in the fall.

Ann felt the house really needed work! She told Jim that he could take over the cleaning, scrubbing, cooking, washing, firing the furnace, cutting the grass, digging weeds, nursing children, ironing clothes to his heart's content. She would take a holiday if there was enough left of her to move! The war was taking its toll on her.

It may really happen some day

For all these reasons, she was hopeful the war would end soon. The news was encouraging. "All the people Florence wished for a safe return at the New Year's Eve party have returned besides you. Maybe you will be along one of these days. Although, I have a feeling you would like to see this thing finished before coming home. It is so hot my arm will scarcely come unstuck from the desk so goodnight sweet prince."

As the summer came to a close, Jim relayed his love in an anniversary note.

"Fourteen years ago, Mr. Pooh caught Mrs. Pooh by her curly locks and dragged her off to his den. Since that time, Mr. Pooh has mostly sat contently in front of said den. He has accepted the praises of the multitudes on what a wonderful den he had, what wonderful food he ate, and what marvelous cubs he had.

"Recently Mr. Pooh took off on the greatest bear junket in history and something remarkable happened. People began writing him and little birds told him that his den was more wonderful than ever. The food was more delicious. The cubs were more amazing than had been in his benign presence.

"Mr. Pooh sat down under an olive tree and nibbled on a piece of dehydrated honey and began to think. It is very remarkable when a male bear thinks. Mr. Pooh did more than just think. He arrived at a CONCLUSION.

Mrs. Pooh is the quintessence of everything beautiful and sweet and wise in the lives of the bear family. Her dynamic influence has caused the most remarkable progeny. You have to admit, when it comes to selecting a wife, the best damn picker in the world is your Mr. Pooh."

It may really happen someday

Other thoughts on Jim's mind concerned his missing comrades. As the number of POWs increased, attention turned to their rescue. The Air Crew Rescue Unit (ACRU) was an important aspect of the Fifteenth Air Force. General Twining and General Eaker set up the rescue apparatus to organize and conduct air crew rescue operations in June 1944. From November 1942 until the close of the action in the Mediterranean, officially May 8, 1945, 28,178 U.S. Airmen were reported missing in action and little organized effort was made to recover them until halfway into the war. These dangerous rescue missions required flying into enemy territory to deliver supplies and aid captured soldiers. Within four months, at the end of October 1944, the ACRU rescued 3,570 Twelfth and Fifteenth evaders as well as many from the Eighth Air Force, the RAF and other Allies.

Col. George Kraigher, a Yugoslav-born American, a pilot in the Serbian Air Force in World War I, and a chief pilot for Pan American Airways, was familiar with the topography of the Balkans. He also knew Marshal Tito, the leader of the Partisans, which was often regarded as the most effective resistance movement in occupied Europe. Kraigher flew 45 missions in C-47s and B-25s to drop supplies or land on secret airfields deep in enemy territory. He played a primary role in "Operation Reunion," a mass recovery operation of downed U.S. crewmen in Rumania. Jim helped determine the locations of POWs based on his knowledge of downed planes.

"Operation Reunion" took place on August 31, 1944. The evacuation was carried out by 36 B-17s. Plywood floors were fitted in the bomb bays and planes flew with five crew, minimum ammunition and no parachutes. Planes arrived in flights of 12 with one hour between flights.

The flights had a heavy fighter escort and other fighters scoured the skies north for the flight path. More than 1,000 jubilant POWs swarmed onto the sunbaked runways and were immediately swept into a whirl of equally excited news photographers, war correspondents, interrogators, high-ranking officers and surprised bystanders. Jim welcomed his fellow comrades.

Many of the recovered POWs were saved and many more helped by the heroic efforts of Princess Catherine Caradja of Rumania, beginning with the August 1, 1943 Ploesti mission. During the war, she aided over 1,000 downed airmen. In addition, through her foundation, St. Catherine's Crib, she aided over 3,000 children.

September 1944 began with accolades for the 376th's completion of 333 bombing missions as reported in the Liberando News Record. The oldest unit in the European-African Middle Eastern Theatre of Operations had an enviable record that, at this point, was twice cited by President Roosevelt. The group currently led the 15th Air Force in precision bombing.

Richard W. Fellows, Lt. Col. A.C. Commanding, acknowledged the bomb groups' accomplishments with a pictorial memorial and the following address:

"For over two and a half years, the Liberandos performed in combat service with distinction. The credit for this performance was due to the flying men and your predecessors who overcame every hazard of combat and enemy opposition to set new standards of bombing accuracy; and to the ground men who successfully coped with all but impossible living and working conditions in adverse weather ranging from the heat and sand of the Western desert to the rain and mud of Italy.

"At the present time, the 376th was not only the oldest heavy Bombardment Group in combat in the European- African- Middle East Theatre but owing to your courage, your perseverance and your high esprit, is the top bombing unit in the Air Force according to actual statistics. To every officer and man, I say "Well Done". To the ex-Liberandos, who passed on to us our proud heritage, I express our sincere gratitude. To the memory of the men of the 376th who gave their lives in the service of their country, I dedicate this pictorial history."

By the end of September, Jim had contracted typhoid fever, a life-threatening illness caused by contaminated food or water. With his positive attitude, he pushed through with this set-back and continued his responsibilities as usual. There was still much work to be done to reach the goal and return to the bear den. As he comments in a letter home,

"Another day nearer to coming home regardless of how far off it may be. There is no need to hold up on sending a Christmas package. Don't send much or make it elaborate as gosh knows where I may be. You might send a pillow. My pillow will be pretty dirty by Christmas. Such things are not attainable

here. Of course, if I start moving, the luxury isn't worth the bother. I got thinking about work after war the other day and drew a few pictures."

Major Jim became the Executive Officer of the 513th Squadron and was instrumental in planning and carrying out the next goal of the 376th Group. The Mediterranean Allied Air Forces (MAAF) main objective during the fall of 1944 was to block and destroy the German forces attempting to evacuate Greece and the rest of the Balkans. Initial attacks by the Fifteenth in September were directed at rail communication targets along the line of the Orient

Express, the lines between Paris, France and Istanbul, Turkey. The MAAF sent 1,400 heavy bomber sorties and the British-commanded Balkan Air Force dispatched 600, delivering heavy blows on the German escape routes.

A nice diversion occurred when the 376th hosted a British parachute commando unit. Their tent camp was raised with military precision in a far corner of San Pan in only a few hours. A few South Africans in the unit performed a Dance of the Zulu Warrior, an impressive physically demanding routine with acrobatic movements. The paratroopers won a soccer match handily, while the 376th hammered them in a softball game, which Jim organized. The unit departed to participate in a highly successful attack on Araxos Airfield, Greece. They contributed to the operations in Greece and by the end of October, that country was entirely occupied by the Allies.

More missions were flown in November than any other month although the weather was not favorable. The Fifteenth introduced a new technique called "Lone Wolf," utilizing radar equipped aircraft in bad weather. The object of these missions was to keep around the clock pressure on the enemy in Vienna, Austria and other surrounding areas. The missions were usually flown by a column of single aircraft hitting a target at ten-minute intervals. Their few bombs were disruptive but their major damage was psychological. The sorties triggered city wide air raid drills which sent thousands of workmen to air raid shelters, causing production delays and sending the message that the AAF was a constant menace in both good and foul weather.

Subsequently, a new Fifteenth Air Force bombing policy was enunciated. No unassigned targets would be struck in Italy except communication targets between the Brenner Pass and Trento-Bassano. Any military targets could be struck in Germany.

Another important rescue mission, Operation Freedom, took place on September 15, 1944. The 47th Wing coordinated a mass evacuation of liberated Fifteenth Air Force combat crews from Cairo to Italy. Long rows of ambulances met the six B-24s and transferred the sick and injured. Strangely missing was the joy; the occasion was very solemn. The POW faces betrayed the tell-tale signs of suffering from the mistreatment, the illnesses, and the unmentionable filth in their Bulgarian prison camps. However, Jim was happy to see some of his fellow soldiers who were left behind in Africa as he grieved the loss of a fun friend, "Swami piccolo."

Lt. "Legs" Diamond was celebrating the end of his tour. He had a short sidekick as a tall boy always seems to have. Before the men, nicknamed "Swami granda" and "Swami piccolo," went on a mission they would wrap towels around their heads and gaze into an electric light bulb and foresee that all would go well. Once the stars were wrong and they buried "Swami Piccolo." Jim had fond memories of joking around with "Swami Piccolo."

Jim realized how fortunate he was to have survived so far and thought often of his family. His correspondence home included apologies for not writing. His excuse was a busted generator and no electric lights. "In my first year, I wrote by candlelight in a dust storm or a flood that didn't respect tents. Now that I am in comfortable quarters, I don't write if the power fails. How spoiled I have become!"

He confessed of an anticipated crime, spending $50 to help build a stone house. The Squadron Commanding Officer Major George asked Jim to join him in building a house out of stone from a nearby building being torn down. "You could say that your husband is a property owner in Italy. If Armistead

Peter (Walter Peter's brother) mentioned his chateau on Lake Cuomo, I could say, 'Oh yes, I had a small place in Italy.'"

While Jim was building a house in moderately warm Italy, Ann reported that it was very cold in Washington, D.C. so the boys went ice skating. The Christmas season was low key and saw little "drop-ins" instead of parties. Ann hosted a New Year's Eve party for the Beale cousins (the Leahys, the Marshalls, and the Bennetts) and a few friends.

The 376th was the first American air group to attack the German/Italian axis. One fighter pilot, Lt. John A, McKean, shared knowledge he gained from being with the outfit. He said, "With the 376th we had the good fortune to draw on the experience of a battle-hardened outfit; a scarce resource in 1943. I remember clearly learning of a means of dealing with a damaged hydraulic system while playing poker with some Old Hands, which saved us later from a certain crash. Such valuable knowledge was absorbed by a form of mental osmosis when surrounded by seasoned campaigners. In a bomber squadron there was a tribal sense of familial support and concern, a togetherness, a bonding that holds to this day." Jim realized the importance of a feeling of connection and was instrumental in creating that atmosphere in his squadron.

Sometimes there were issues with the Allies that had to be resolved. As the Russians moved through the Balkans in closer proximity to the Americans, it became increasingly difficult for the Fifteenth to work with them because the Russians insisted that the bomb lines be established in Moscow. General Eaker, through the Moscow Military Mission Chief, General John R. Deane, notified the Russians that as of December 3, 1944, MAAF would operate west of a line he would designate and change daily. The line would include the main routes used by the retreating Germans but would be far enough from the Russians to protect them. Ultimately, the Russians agreed to Eaker's unilateral action. Deane wrote, "The Russians... had much more respect for us and acquiesced more readily when we simply informed them that 'this is what we are going to do – take it or leave it.' There is merit in considering adherence to similar procedure in the future."

After months of optimistic progress reports on the Allied ground successes in Europe, word of the German Ardennes break-through on December 16th brought gloom and discouragement to the Liberandos with the certain knowledge that the war was far from over. Although this would be the last great German offensive, it was not apparent at the time. It looked more like another Dunkirk, the evacuation of Allied troops in France in 1940.

The Liberandos never let their disappointment interfere with their duties. The day after Christmas, the 376th continued the fight with five consecutive attacks on the Brenner Pass targets, the jugular vein of the Nazi forces in Italy. By the end of the year, the Brenner Pass had been blocked. In addition, communications, oil, and industrial targets in the Vienna area were heavily bombed.

The spirited Liberandos celebrated their accomplishments with the "Olive Bowl" game of touch football on New Year's Day. The 376th Lib Flyers met the 47th Wing Dings. Large red numbers were sewn on GI uniforms to distinguish the teams. Pools of water dotted the field with freezing temperatures. The game was played in true American style and effort, including cheerleaders and a brass band. The thrilling game ended in a 7-7 tie. A fun, competitive sporting event gave the Liberandos a positive start to 1945 – the year the war would finally come to an end.

Chapter 11
The Last Five Yards

Ann shared with Jim that she hosted the 1945 New Year's Eve celebration with singing led by Dick Marshall and Billy Leahy. The gang was most interested in all the details of Jim's life in Italy. Everybody noted that Jim, the life of a party, was missing and they looked forward to his presence at the next New Year's Eve gathering. "It's hard to realize that another year is beginning and you are still far from home but at least the new year gives me hope that before another year rolls around it will all be over and our lives settled once more."

Little Ann enjoyed a few days with her grandparents. The boys were ready to return to school and the Greene family would brace for the hardest part of winter. They were all well and Ann prayed that good health would continue. For the new year, she hoped to see families united and a start toward lasting peace all over the world.

From his post at San Pan, Italy, Jim reported that his health was excellent but he was overwhelmed with paperwork. "I just wasn't cut out for an administrative clerk or garrison duty. The more I see of different conditions of warfare and troop psychology the more I'm convinced that the American soldier is at his best under the worst conditions if he is properly led. It takes so much to make us mad that unless you put us on 'C' rations, kick us in a mud hole or a dust storm and drop a few bombs on our heads we get more interested in comfortable living, satisfying inspectors and wondering when the war will end than we do in destroying the other people." Jim thought that human beings were not naturally aggressive and didn't want to fight but, if necessary, they would rise to the task.

Day-by-day living conditions and facilities improved, but the inspectors got more critical, resulting in endless paperwork. Fortunately, the weather was much drier than the previous year. Jim put a blanket up on the door and had a stove going full blast so his room was comfortable. He seemed to feel a bit guilty of his pleasant surroundings, so he requested a transfer to a more dangerous fighting role but was denied.

The boys on the other side of the Apennines Mountain range were catching the bad weather. On the warfront, Jim hoped the Russians could distinguish the Americans from the Italians if they got to his base. "Maybe we expect too much of them, but the Russians have never failed us yet."

At the end of 1944, there were 3,359,000 soldiers with 1,100,000 men serving overseas and 41,000 aircraft in the United States and 31,000 planes and bombers overseas. General Eisenhower believed that the strategic air offensive was having a catastrophic effect on the German economy by early 1945. The remarkable success of attacks on oil resulted in a crisis in German transportation and all phases of the German industrial effort, with direct impact on the ground battle.

As a result of these accomplishments, General Henry H. "Hap" Arnold, commanding general of the United States Army Air Forces, reduced the pilot training rate from 105,000 men per year in the fall of 1944 to 30,000 by February 1945. Although the war was still an all-out worldwide conflict, General Arnold slowed aircraft production and cancelled aircraft orders totaling $7 billion. The upper echelon believed a victory was in sight.

However, the Liberandos saw a different picture. The December Nazi advance in the Ardennes in Belgium, Germany, and France, was very discouraging. The ground fighting was stalled on the Gothic Line which was German Field Marshal Albert Kesseling's last major line of defense along the summits of the northern part of the Apennine Mountains in Italy. The Russian advances had slowed down in the east. It looked like the war was neither getting easier nor coming to an end.

While the war continued, the Liberandos celebrated another Mediterranean Theatre flying record in January. The *Boomerang,* a B-24 Liberator, completed 132 flying missions traveling 198,000 miles in ten months. The B-24 Liberator dropped over 600,000 pounds of bombs, hitting some of the hottest targets in Europe, Ploesti, Vienna, Munich and Budapest.

One of February's highlights was the completion of the Liberandos' 400th mission. General Rush, commander of the 47th Bombardment Wing of the Fifteenth Air Force, commented that the 376th Bombardment Group participated more definitively and extensively toward an ultimate defeat of the enemy. "The record of this veteran group with many commendations and citations, identifies it as one of the truly great units of the United States Army Air Force."

Concentrating on Austria, the Liberandos continued their assault, participating in a massive attack on railyards, stations, grade crossings, barges, docks, signal centers, tracks and bridges. Most of these targets in small cities had never been attacked. Operation CLARION took place on February 22nd, involving over 6,000 Allied aircraft from the RAF, and the United States Eighth, Ninth, Twelfth, and Fifteenth Air Forces. The Liberandos' focus was the railyards in southern Germany. The Allied bombing insured that German fighting would come to an end.

In the midst of the intensified war activities, Ann sent a cable notifying Jim of his stepfather's death. She also forwarded a letter from a lawyer informing him that his stepfather had remembered him in his will. Jim gave Ann full power of attorney. He supposed Uncle Sam would take a big cut out of the inheritance, which was right and proper. Jim felt that he should contribute a share of his good fortune to help support the country. Jim responded to the sad news of the loss of his stepfather with these thoughts, "I was mighty fond of Walter and know I have lost a good friend. Gosh, everybody I know is getting grown up or dying. It'll be like starting off in a new city."

It may really happen some day

Jim contributed as much as he could during his squadron's bond selling competition. Soldiers purchased war bonds as another way to support the war effort. Participation in the competition meant that he sent Mrs. Pooh $125 in bonds instead of cash as a result of all the "racket." The bonds were an investment, but gave Ann less cash as she had to wait for them to mature. Perhaps as a consolation, he included a Valentine poem in his correspondence to her:

> I've crossed the sandy desert,
> And snowy mountains too
> But I find I'm always dreaming
> of my darling Mrs. Pooh.
> I've flown the mighty oceans,
> Saw continents a few,
> But no sight so rare as could compare
> With my lovely Mrs. Pooh.
>
> And when the war is over
> And Uncle says, "You're through"
> No more I'll roam, I'm coming home
> To my own Mrs. Pooh!

Ann shed a tear as she read the sweet poem and was relieved to receive some correspondence as she hadn't heard from Jim in a while. She had previously mentioned her wish for the Russians to hurry up and take Berlin since Mr. Pooh couldn't fly and help take it himself. Jim made Ann a promise--that he wouldn't fly over Berlin. "I'd be court martialed immediately, and if I got shot down there would be no compensation for Mrs. Pooh. I'm not figuring on stowing away."

Ann was busy tending to her mother who was convalescing from pneumonia. Her recovery was because of the new wonder drug, penicillin. The antibiotic was discovered in 1928 and started being used to cure infections in 1942. It was a major breakthrough in treating many illnesses. The Ration Board gave Ann an extra five gallons of gas to make trips to the hospital. She was normally allowed 1.5 gallons a week. Aside from controlling the amount of gas, rationing had a major impact on wartime diets. "Meat was very scarce; we almost never have bacon anymore. Managed to get a little ground beef today for a meatloaf. Don't know when I've had a steak! We have plenty of everything except meat, butter, and cheese."

Ann wrote that she received money from Aunt Florence to buy a lily to take to the cemetery and place it on Jim's grandmother's grave. She thought it would be nice to visit Florence in South Carolina, but she couldn't get the gas to drive. Ann hoped Jim would get to Algiers to visit his friend Sam's grave. As the war in Europe was nearing an end, Ann wondered if Jim would come home or go to the Pacific Theatre.

Spring arrived in Italy with olive trees in bloom. The warm weather meant a great and unprecedented push by Allied land armies in both the east and west. The Nazis temporarily stalled the British and American forces in its desperate Bulge counterattack, and the Russians pulled up to Warsaw and stopped. The stage was being set for the final thrust.

The tempo of the war reached a crescendo due to the fair weather, allowing for safe air travel. Any massive frontal attack by ground armies was preceded by heavy bomber and fighter attacks. More than half of the 376th March missions were in support of the Russian offensive, steadily pushing toward the Austrian border.

The Liberandos looked to a future with hope and optimism. Their morale was soaring.

Large formations of Liberators were no longer needed. Good targets became scarce because of their successful raids. For example, Vienna was one of the most heavily defended targets in Europe. After almost seven months, the

Liberandos made their 47th and final trip on March 22, 1945. No German refineries were able to produce gasoline within the operations range of the Fifteenth Air Force.

Constant bombing greatly reduced the marshalling traffic on the main Linz, Munich, and Regensburg route. The American armies crossed the Rhine in the west and took thousands of German prisoners. Meanwhile, Russia began its last assault on Berlin. Germany's few holdings in the Balkans were also strangled. In northern Italy, the American Fifth and the British Eighth ground to a stop.

Jim accepted a last-minute opportunity and traveled to Paris for a few days. Some areas of France were devastated by the war, but not much of downtown Paris. He shared his observations with Ann: "I'm sitting in the sunshine listening to tinkling fountains and sniffing beautiful flowers and feeling very much like Ferdinand the Bull [1]. It certainly is a beautiful spot, though I must admit I can't enjoy it as much as I should for thinking of old Sam and the days of our trip to Europe almost 20 years ago."

Jim continued his description of a part of Paris that seemed hardly touched by the war. The people were clean and well-dressed and happily strolled about with cute kids and elaborate baby buggies. All the shops were very ritzy and dressed up with evening clothes, leather goods, and jewelry. The prices were outlandish! A nice pocketbook cost more than the $50 Jim had in his pocket. He went to a swank nightclub which was "In Bounds" and prices were controlled; the other places were expensive. Soldiers, Red Cross girls, and American nurses bought drinks for $1 and a bottle of champagne for $13. "Incidentally, you can feel very sure of my virtue as I understand the many beautiful ladies who hover about have a minimum charge of $40 for an evening's entertainment and as far as I can see there is no unemployment."

While relaxing on a park bench, he saw a couple of well-dressed Frenchmen who looked at him curiously and felt they were trying to figure out how to charge him for sitting in their city, maybe with some kind of sunshine meter and rate per tinkle of the fountain. The French were very creative at making a franc. The women were the most attractive of any country in the world. Therefore, he recommended that France be on the U.S. side in all future wars.

---

[1] Ferdinand the Bull was a popular children's book about a bull who would rather smell flowers than fight in a bull ring.

"At my age it's obvious that I'm only thinking of the welfare of the succeeding generations."

He daydreamed that it would be lovely if the Pooh family sat in a row dozing with him. But when reality set in he thought that the Pie Pooh would fall in the fountain, Jimmy would fall off a bicycle, and Billy would fall off the roof and need many stitches. Then Mrs. Pooh would kiss everybody including Mr. Pooh, and all would go happily to dinner. Jim had to be content with walking to a café and enjoying delicious French cuisine.

The next day Jim drove to the coast and walked down to the beach. Along with many other spectators he watched German prisoners clearing the old harbor defenses. He made a large sand bear for some French children. After a while he strolled toward the boardwalk. He noticed a pretty young French girl sitting on the seawall and timidly gravitated toward her. Her mother suddenly spoke up, "You are in aviation, aren't you?" She broke the ice. The woman knew enough English and Jim knew enough French to carry on a pleasant conversation. He shared the children's pictures which seemed to delight the French women. The trip was a bright spot in a tedious existence.

Wherever Jim was, on base or on leave, home seemed very far away. Jim felt he would be like a stranger to those he knew in the past and that he would have to get reacquainted all over again. Everyone seemed dim and remote, and conjured up in his mind from long ago. "It's difficult to explain but with people marrying and dying and kids growing up, you just feel you're not a part of the group you used to belong to and therefore it's hard to believe they could be interested in you."

The
LETTER
(Uncensored)

Frontispiece –

PORTRAIT OF
THE AUTHOR

By Ann Greene WAC

Chapter I

A GOOD WAC NEVER NEGLECTS HER DUTY — SO I AM GOING TO WRITE TO MY DADDY

Chapter II

"DEAR DADDY" THIS IS GOING TO BE A NICE L-O-N-G LETTER

Chapter III

GOSH! WHAT DO YOU SAY TO A GUY YOU DONT EVEN KNOW?

Chapter IV

I FINALLY FINISHED IT - SO NOW I'LL MAIL IT O-O-O! LOOK AT THE BIG AUTOMOBILE.

Chapter V

WHY-HELLO GENERAL! SURE I'D APPRECIATE A LIFT.

Chapter VI

AND THATS THE END OF THE STORY OF THE LETTER. OH, THE GENERAL? THATS ANOTHER STORY.

April 1945 was an historic month for the 376th Bomb Group. The word "home" overshadowed all other events. The first electrifying rumors of the end of the war started to circulate early in the month and blossomed into an almost unbelievable fact on VE Day, May 8, 1945.

Spring came to Washington, D.C. and Ann was happy to see irises and roses showing their foliage. She placed pussy willows on the dining room table. Most of the flower beds had grown over since Jim wasn't there to tend them. He had been away for four springs now. Ann arranged for needed repair work on the house. She focused on the necessary maintenance, like repairing screens, painting the porch, and replacing a few shingles on the roof. The costs were high and the workmanship was inferior. She wished Jim was home to help her.

The children were happy playing baseball and roller skating. Little Ann was excited about her first hopscotch game. Bill had his first date and took his girlfriend to a movie. Jim took his girlfriend to the basketball game. "It's good they can earn money for their social life since they begin so young!" "Big" Ann and Jim had gone to single-sex colleges and didn't go on dates until after graduation. They married in their early thirties after most of their friends, having made plans for their wedding in 1930 before the effects of the Depression postponed their and many other nuptials.

Sadly, before the war came to an end, President Roosevelt died on April 12th. General Twining broadcast the following message to his command, "I express the feeling of every officer, man and woman of the United States Fifteenth Army Air Force when I express my organization's regret at the untimely death of our great leader and commander-in-chief, President Franklin Delano Roosevelt; the absence of whose wise and able leadership will be sorely missed by the people of the United States, its Armed Forces and by all democratic peoples throughout the world. Let us, as we face the problems of the coming peace, remember the lessons which he taught us throughout the difficult years of his service to humanity."

Even though the European war's end was near, the daily aerial combat continued.

Operation APPLE was launched on April 9th and began the final ground offensive on the Italian front. It was concurrent with a drive by the French forces on the French Italian border. The Eighth Army drove toward Argenta in northern Italy. The Allied Forces took Bologna, Italy, on April 21st, 1945. These drives finally ended on May 2nd when the Germans surrendered.

Mission 451, flown on April 15th, 1945, was the Liberandos' last combat assignment. The weary 376th, part of the Fifteenth Air Force, participated in the largest air operation ever conducted. WOWSER was the air phase of the ground breakthrough at Bologna. All 1,235 flyable heavy bombers (98%) in the Fifteenth Air Force blasted German troop concentrations, gun positions, and strong points facing Allied ground troops. The Strategic Air War was over.

General Twining concluded that the war in the European Theatre had been won. He praised the Fifteenth Air Force's accomplishments by saying: "Such deeds are not attained by waving a magic wand or by use of Aladdin's lamp, but by hard work, loyalty, and a conscientious devotion to duty of the entire Force. I am greatly impressed by the effort put forth by the Fifteenth service command and the ground echelons of all units, without which such a tempo of operations would be impossible. This, with the expert planning by the organization staffs and the courage and skill of the air crews, rounded out the team that enables this Air Force to attain the highest degree of effectiveness."

Due to the success of the 47th organization, they were selected for redeployment through the United States and then they would be sent to finish the job against Japan with the use of the B-29 Fortresses. This signal honor was a tribute to the unprecedented achievements of the 47th Wing throughout its two and a half years of campaigning in the Middle East, Africa, and Italy.

The war in Europe was over, but the Liberandos' work was not finished. They were scheduled to convert to flying B-29s, relocate to Okinawa, and join the Eighth Air Force against Japan. They sailed from Taranto, Italy, on the plush *USS West Point* on April 19, 1945.

Fear was still being incited via the radio. Mildred Gillers, a turncoat American from Conneault, Ohio, joined the Hitler team while in Germany in 1934. After the war, she was brought back to America, tried for treason and spent 12 years in prison. She died on June 25, 1988 at the age of 87. She was "Axis Sally" on the airways and at the end of April 1945, with only days left in the war, she sent this message from Berlin, trying to frighten the troops with conspiracy theories.

"You boys are so gullible and so trusting. You are happy tonight because you think Colonel Warren is taking you home to your wives and sweethearts. Well, I'm sorry fellows, because you will never see your homes again. You'll never see Brooklyn, Texas, or California. Listen to this, boys. From the moment you board the *USS West Point* at Taranto, you will be watched. You will be followed by our underseas boats which never miss their target like you fellows often did. Your position at sea will be known to us every minute. Either the first or second night out of Gibraltar – yes, it will happen late at night – you will be torpedoed without a trace and won't have a chance to fight back. It will be a kind of death different from what you escaped in the air over southern Europe.

"While you are struggling for survival in the freezing waters of the cold North Atlantic, just think of your dear wives and sweethearts; think how they will grieve for you for a few days, collect your insurance, and then step out again with their 4-F boyfriends who took your place while you were fighting the German people who were never your real enemies."

The Liberandos heard enough of Sally's propaganda to remember that some of her ominous predictions were borne out. Just enough came true that, although this warning was laughed off as mere hot air, she did raise some concern about the homeward bound cruise. Not one 376th soldier tried to get off the return list. On the contrary, many crew members were disappointed that they were ordered to remain in Italy.

Axis Sally's warning did not cancel plans for a "going home" celebration by the Liberandos on the night of her predictions. They made a huge pile of five-gallon gas cans each filled with a quart of gasoline topped with scraps of lumber. They laid a gasoline trail from the heap of cans off to a spot some 200 feet away. After dark, a lighted match was touched to the trail. Slowly it snaked its way toward the pile of containers. A whoosh of fire lit up the heavens with periodic explosions as the gas cans became heated. All went well until one of the overheated, cans sailed through the air and alighted on the roof of Colonel Warren's sleeping quarters where he was making a final check on shipping papers. Fortunately, no serious damage occurred, and all enjoyed the celebration.

The most distasteful last-minute duty was saying good-bye to the 14 remaining Yugoslav Royal Air Force Detachment crewmen who had to stay behind. President Roosevelt had presented four B-24Js to the flyers at Bolling Field, Washington, D.C. on October 6, 1943. The Yugoslav flying personnel were attached to the 376th Bombardment Group in Enfidaville, Tunisia for the remainder of the war. On July 23, 1947, the United States passed Indiana Senator William E. Jenner's bill providing for naturalization of the Yugoslav airmen.

On April 18, 1945, Jim notified Ann, effective immediately and until further notice, not to send any more mail to him at the current address. He would advise as soon as possible when mail could be resumed. His pre-embarkation health certificate found him to be free from communicable and quarantinable diseases, free from vermin, and complying with current War Department immunization requirements for military. Jim was required to keep this certification with him at all times. His bags were packed for his journey across the Atlantic and back to the United States.

The USS West Point, the battleship gray queen of the American Merchant Marine, was docked in Bari Harbor and ready to ferry 7,500 soldiers. The ship played a tremendous role in the nation's war effort, transporting 350,000 troops around the world without a casualty. The biggest merchant vessel ever constructed in an American shipyard, intended for the elite North Atlantic passenger service, was transformed into a battleship.

The 376th and the 98th Bomb Groups, together with headquarters and two squadrons of the 62nd Air Service Group, embarked on April 18th. The Fifteenth Air Force band played steadily until every man, dragging his souvenir laden barracks bag, was on board. The only difficulty was encountered when a small boat overloaded with excess baggage, official records, and supplies sank to the bottom of the harbor. The valuable and irreplaceable history of many missions was far beyond restoration. Some hours after the ship sailed it was revealed that 22 dogs had been secretly stowed. All the pets made it safely to the United States. The ship made a secure voyage across the Atlantic Ocean and landed at the Norfolk Naval Station in Virginia on April 29, 1945. Axis Sally had been mistaken.

Jim spent his 30-day furlough getting reacquainted with his family before he rejoined the Liberandos. He played basketball and pitched a few baseballs to Jimmy and Bill. He helped Ann with spring cleaning and getting the porch ready for summer. He spent a few hours taking in the familiar smells of the neighborhood and caught up with neighbors. The extended family got together to celebrate little Ann's belated birthday and his safe return.

Jim arrived in Nebraska on June 9, 1945. A select group of old Liberandos and some new members had assembled at Geneva Air Force Base in late May. The 512th, 513th, and 514th squadrons of the 376th Heavy Bombardment Group moved to Grand Island, Nebraska, for B-29 transition training. The B-24 Liberator group prepared to fly the B-29 Superfortress.

Jim became the executive officer and commander of troops of the 514th Squadron. All pilots qualified on the B-29s and the entire Group passed the Preparation for Overseas Movement with top grades in all departments. By August 15th, the Liberandos were ready to go to their assignment in the Pacific.

The first atomic bomb was dropped on Japan on August 6th. Russia entered the Far East battle and the Japanese Empire called it quits. These events threw the 376th Heavy Bombardment Group into a frenzy of joy. However, the Group still planned to go to the Pacific Theatre as scheduled. Its readiness date was August 25th.

Just when it appeared the Liberandos were seaward bound, rumors started to run rampant. The Port of Embarkation was holding up all equipment. On September 5th, General Rush made the solemn announcement that the 47th Wing and the 376th, "were no more." Their job was well done.

On August 23rd, Ann and Jim remembered their fourth anniversary apart. Jim's present was a surprise phone call telling her that he would be home soon. The next day, Ann wrote to Jim, "Just can't begin to tell you how happy I was after your phone call last night. Had been feeling pretty low all day, fearing you might have to go to the Pacific anyway. I'm sure everything will turn out for the best and no matter what hard times may be in store, at least we will be together.

"Your letter with the drawings arrived in the mail yesterday morning. We surely timed our greetings to each other nicely. The drawings were darling. I love them. Can hardly believe it's really true that you will be coming home for good. It will certainly be wonderful and the thought really 'peps me up!' With hearts full of love from all your poohs – most from your Mrs. Pooh."

Jim's focus turned to securing employment when he returned to Washington, D.C. The commercial art firm he helped co-found had replaced him during the war, therefore he wasn't guaranteed a position. He sent a letter asking Ann to contact his partner in the business. Ann reported, "I will mail him your request and let him reply directly to you. I have no comment to make: you will have to make decisions yourself and whatever you decide will have to work somehow or other. I'll just do the best I can in any circumstances."

Jim flew home with other personnel headed to Army Air Force Headquarters on September 11, 1945. After a joyous reunion with his family, there were several gatherings welcoming him home. In addition, Jim participated in many parades in surrounding communities. He appreciated the accolades but was humbled by the wounded soldiers, particularly Billy's emaciated peewee football coach who had survived the Bataan Death March. The coach, while sitting on a convertible, had to be held up by two friends. Many of his circle never returned from the war. Jim remembered his childhood friend, Sam, and many other friends who lost their lives. For the rest of his life, he stayed in touch with Sam's son.

Most importantly, Daddy Bear was now present in the lives of his busy teenage sons, attending their sporting events and other activities. He loved being a part of their lives and cheering for them at their games. Daddy Bear had a great time getting to know his four-year-old daughter, Pie Pooh. The children were ecstatic to have their father home to play with them. They listened attentively as he told stories of his many adventures. Jim did his best to put the past behind him and live in the present for the sake of his family.

Fortunately, though he was not guaranteed a position, Jim was able to rejoin the commercial art firm, which had barely stayed in business while he was away. Promptly, he worked diligently to expand it. He went on the road to reestablish prewar accounts, a very different routine than the one he had been living. Advertising of personal and home use items helped the business. Once again, five years later, Ann and Jim faced a momentous personal decision.

When the Korean War broke out, Jim was asked to reenter the military and serve stateside. Jim's essential character was manifested in patriotic service to his country. As soon as his sons graduated from high school, Jim resigned from the Walter-Hoke commercial art firm located in Washington, D.C. and

Baltimore, Maryland. At the time, he was the vice president and the treasurer of the company he had co-founded in 1930. Ann and Jim moved to Camp Hill, Pennsylvania, in 1952 so that Jim could work for the Selective Service System in Harrisburg, Pennsylvania, during the Korean War. As a staff officer, he helped locate draftees who did not report for duty.

However, there was one mystery that still tormented Jim at the end of the war, the fate of the bomber, *Lady Be Good*. The airplane was found in the desert in 1958. The inconceivable story of the devasting last days of the survivors follows.

Chapter 12
Incomprehensible

In 1958, Jim received astounding news. The remains of the *Lady Be Good* B-24 bomber were spotted during an oil exploration trip in the African desert. Jim had been the intelligence officer of the 514th squadron at the time of the plane's disappearance, and he had spent hours investigating the bomber's whereabouts. This new information stirred up all the memories of that fateful time. Jim remembered every soldier who was in his squadron, especially these men who were lost.

On April 4, 1943, shortly after Jim arrived at Berka 2 near Soluch, he agreed at the last minute to fly with his tentmate, Lt. Worley, as a replacement for an ailing bombardier on the Naples, Italy, attack. The mission led to one of World War II's legendary mysteries, the disappearance of the 514th Squadron plane, the *Lady Be Good.*

Between June 12, 1942 and April 15, 1945, the 376th Heavy Bombardment Group and its parent organization lost 169 aircraft in combat. In almost every case, crew members were also lost, inevitably under tragic circumstances. The planes were written off and replaced, the men were mourned and buried when their remains could be recovered, and the war went on. The significance of losing any particular plane and its crew was largely unremarkable taken in the context of winning a global war. There was nothing at the time to suggest that the disappearance of this plane would become a World War II legend.

The saga of the *Lady be Good* began on an ominous day. Twenty-five planes left mid-afternoon in clouds of sand. The abrasive sand particles compromised some of the aircrafts' carburetors and spark plugs. Engine problems and frozen face masks caused 14 planes to drop out of the action. Undetected strong northeasterly winds at high altitude caused the remaining planes to drift west and south of the briefed route. During this period, missions flown against targets on Sicily and in Italy were without a fighter escort. Consequently, to minimize the period of engagement with enemy fighters and exposure to anti-aircraft batteries over enemy territory, the formations were timed to arrive over the target at sundown after remaining away from enemy coastlines as long as possible. On this day, the second group of planes, led by the *Lady Be Good,* arrived after dark, so they decided to turn back. Lt. Worley's plane and two other planes followed in formation.

In marginal weather, locating their home airfield at Soluch at night was a challenge for navigators. They often had to resort to celestial navigation plus they needed to confirm their position estimates with fixes obtained by the radio operators aboard their planes. Within 50 miles, they could home in on a low-powered transmitter positioned near Soluch if the weather conditions were favorable. Additionally, a light beacon was located nearby. But because the water and shoreline appeared similar to the desert sand, crews could easily miss the coast and continue into the desolate Libyan Desert.

To relieve the stress of flying close formation and minimize the hazard of mid-air collisions, the formations loosened up. Ten planes returned with massive damage from enemy flak. The four planes led by the *Lady Be Good* continued to the west coast of Italy and turned toward Soluch. Jim watched the *Lady Be Good* attempt a landing in a blinding sand storm and abort, never to be seen again. The other planes returned safely by 11:30 p.m. even though Jim's plane almost ran out of gas before safely landing.

The next day William McCain, a pilot from the 514th, flew southwest for over 200 miles looking for the missing plane. The aerial search revealed nothing but trackless desert. The RAF Wellington Search and Rescue aircraft made sweeps over the Mediterranean Sea along the return route from Naples and nothing was found. An investigation of the Naples area was made by an officer with the Army's Casualty Clearance Detachment without eliciting any information. The Graves Registration board findings concluded the active interest of the United States government in the search five years later.

Fifteen years after the mission, on November 9, 1958, a geologist, Ronald McLean, spotted a plane resting on a gravel plain 385 miles from Tobruk, Libya, during a survey flight. A closer look revealed a World War II heavy bomber remarkably intact and bearing the white stars against a blue circle of the American Army Air Force. The plane still retained most of its original pink camouflage color.

By the middle of February 1959, geologists had made their way close to where the bomber had been sighted. They stood on the southern edge of a featureless sand and gravel expanse that extended as far as the eye could see. The eerie desolation exceeded anything the men had ever experienced in an occupation that had taken them to the remotest parts of the world. Not a trace of vegetation was visible. The men gasped in the 130-degree superheated air at noon.

Late that afternoon of February 27th, they arrived at the coordinates identified as the location of the American bomber 420 miles southeast of its base at Soluch. The twin vertical stabilizers of the bomber were spotted at 5:30 p.m. The name, *Lady Be Good,* was still visible below the window. On the floor inside were the empty canvas bags used to carry the parachutes, indicating the plane had come down relatively intact. High altitude clothing items remained hanging in place and bore the name tags of their owners. When the life raft compartments were opened, undisturbed rations and cans of water along with a survival radio confirmed the crew and plane had not come down together.

The question that intrigued the public worldwide and tormented the next of kin for another year and a half was what had happened to the crew. There were strong indications that the crew had remained with the plane until fuel exhaustion. They suggested that the crew's bailout would have been within a five-mile radius of the *Lady be Good's* location.

On June 5th, an expedition departed from Benghazi on the sandy Kufra Trail, an ancient caravan route connecting the Kufra Oasis with the Mediterranean coast. The trail, a mile wide in places, gets even wider as vehicles avoid previous tire tracks to avoid bogging down. Arriving at a point 440 miles south of Benghazi, the convoy left the Kufra Trail and turned east to cross the western arm of the Calanscio Sand Sea which was 60 miles wide. The 90-mile trip was a constant struggle navigating 50 to 500-foot dunes. Long perforated strips of steel had to be wedged under the wheels to regain traction in many places.

The gravel plain surrounding the *Lady Be Good* was 18,000 square miles. For six days, a 450-square-mile area with the B-24 at the center, was searched with no luck. Next a three-by-ten-mile rectangle was outlined in the gravel surface 35 miles northwest from the B-24 as that was believed to be the limit the crew could walk in the existing conditions. On June 16th, late in the afternoon of the first day, 19 miles from the *Lady be Good*, a pair of sheepskin boots were found pointing northwest, with electric cords for heated flying suits coiled inside the right boot.

The next major break occurred on June 19th approximately two miles from the boots. An arrowhead-shaped marker fashioned from a parachute, a pair of flight boots, an intact pile of cut parachute shroud lines and the frame of a parachute, a "pilot chute" were found. A complete liner for an electrically-heated flying suit was found a mile and a half farther.

At intervals along the next 15 miles, four more parachute markers and other pieces of flight clothing were found. Just at the sixth marker, there was an intersection of trails. At this point, the searchers returned to Benghazi to regroup for the second phase of the search.

The second expedition left Benghazi on July 10th. The seventh parachute marker was found on July 20th. Ten more markers were found along the crew's 35-mile trek. Due to frequent breakdowns and fuel shortages, it was determined that helicopters were necessary to continue the search.

Two dismantled helicopters were delivered and reassembled at the crash site on August 16th. The helicopters dramatically accelerated the search operations. On August 31st, following final sweeps in the southern reaches of the Sand Sea by the one working helicopter, search operations were terminated. The search party determined that the crew members must have perished in the sand dunes and that their bodies were covered by sand.

In an amazing coincidence, at the same time, Jim suffered a massive heart attack. After ten minutes of no heartbeat, he was declared dead. Miraculously, his heart started beating again. Did the unanswered questions about the *Lady Be Good* and his desire for answers keep him alive?

On February, 11, 1960, an exploration group of geologists were obtaining seismic data from subsurface rock strata at a location 85 miles north/northwest of the *Lady Be Good,* along the southern fringe of the Sand Sea. There they found the closely grouped remains of five of the Lady Be Good crewmen. Sterile surroundings had prevented disturbances of the remains by animals or insects. During the course of studying the scattered clothing, a small reminder-type diary was found in the pocket of a rolled-up pair of flight overalls. Co-pilot Lt. Toner's notes recounted the seven crew members' 78-mile struggle to survive after bailing out.

As a result of these findings, a third search was organized to find the three other crew members. On May 12, 1960, a British Petroleum geophysical party found the sixth airman 26 miles from the other five remains. The seventh soldier, Sgt. Risplinger, walked 115 miles to his death. The third phase search ended with one soldier still missing.

All evidence suggested that after 17 years, the case of the *Lady Be Good* could be closed at last. But fate had one final card to play. On August, 11, 1960, nearly three months after searchers departed, word was received that more human remains had been found. The location was 12 miles northeast of the crash site. Lt. Woravka's failed parachute cause him to fall to his death sparing him the drawn-out suffering of his fellow crew members.

After recovering his body, the British Petroleum Exploration team found the rally point of the other seven crew members four tenths of a mile southwest of the *Lady Be Good*. Concentrated in a small area were clothing, parachutes, and life preservers. Mercifully, they had been unaware that 458 miles lay between them and their base at Soluch.

Their efforts to survive in one of the most hostile environments on earth are deserving of the highest praise and admiration. Five of the men walked 78 miles with only a few drops of water each day. Sgt Ripslinger and Shelley struggled on an additional 26 and 37 miles, respectively. Survival studies indicated that a man walking only at night in the temperatures encountered by Lt. Hatton and his crew would be too weak to continue after less than two days and 25 miles of travel. The *Lady Be Good* crew persevered in their trek for five days while covering over three times the most optimistic distance estimates.

Jim's heart attack precipitated his retirement from the military. He and Ann moved back to Chevy Chase, Maryland, to be near family and long-time friends. During the next ten years, Jim reflected on his military service and its impact on his family. It led him to think about previous generations and decided that he wanted to learn more about his ancestors and their life experiences in the context of U.S. history. This interest called for a few road trips throughout the country, which included visiting old friends.

Chapter 13
A Soldier's Sojourn

After Jim was resuscitated and recovered from his heart attack, he and Ann decided to move from Camp Hill, Pennsylvania, back to Chevy Chase, Maryland, to be close to family and friends. His third and final retirement from the military became effective Oct 1, 1959.

Ann and Jim bought a comfortable two-story brick home in a quiet neighborhood in Chevy Chase. The house was within walking distance of relatives and friends. They enjoyed entertaining and sitting on the screened porch with a view of their rose garden. He was fortunate to fully recover, but he knew another heart attack was possible and could incapacitate him or end his life, so he appreciated every day.

Jim set aside a room in the basement for his war memorabilia from his two years in the European-African-Middle Eastern Theater. It was here that he reflected on his time in the military. Jim understood all too well the words of Rick Atkinson, "There were lessons of camaraderie and duty and inscrutable fate. There were lessons of honor and courage, of compassion and sacrifice." He thought about the wonderful people he met along the way, particularly the many men who sacrificed their lives. He was proud of all they had accomplished while in Africa and Italy and being part of the collective Allied success in stopping the evils of the Nazi regime.

Jim was grateful that he had enough ability and stamina at age 42 to serve his country as part of the United States military and return home in good health. He respected the Allied leadership and its ingenuity, as well as its organizational and collaborative expertise. He knew just how fortunate the United States was in not having to fight a war on its mainland after seeing firsthand the devastation in Africa and Europe. Most importantly, he knew future generations would have a chance to live with the freedoms that he valued and appreciated.

According to his official military records, as explained by Lt. Col. William A. McIntosh, Jim received 13 bronze service stars during the war for the following battles: Tunisia, May 13, 1943, Ploesti, August 1, 1943, Sicily, August 17, 1943, Southern France, September 14,1944, Air Offensive Europe, May 11, 1944, Naples-Foggia, January 21, 1944, Rome-Arno, September 9, 1944, Northern France, September 14, 1944, Normandy, July 24, 1944, and Po Valley, May 8, 1945, Rhineland, March 21, 1945, and North Appenines April 4, 1945.

Jim was presented three Presidential Unit Citations (PUC), the highest unit decoration awarded, tantamount to presenting the Distinguished Service Cross to every member of the unit who served during the period recognized. The citations were awarded for action over Ploesti, Rumania, on August 1, 1943, for action over Tunisia and Sicily, May 1942 – August 17, 1943, and for action over Bratislava, Czechoslovakia, June 16, 1944.

Persons serving with a unit receiving the PUC are entitled to wear the award for the rest of their lives.

Shortly before VE Day, Jim was awarded the Bronze Star Medal on April 15, 1945, for his collective service. As noted, Jim had a keen sense of doing the right thing in extraordinary circumstances. He instinctively improvised when a difficult situation presented itself and he was able to maintain a genial atmosphere with his sense of humor and indominable spirit. Jim had a natural ability to get along with people and he never forgot the importance of protecting those in his charge to the best of his ability. The following citation encapsulates his contribution to the war effort:

Citation

James F. Greene, 0169708, Major, Air Corps, 513th Bombardment Squadron, 376th Bombardment Group (H), United States Army. For meritorious service not involving participation in aerial flight during the period 21 September 1943 thru 21 January 1945. As executive officer of his heavy bombardment squadron, Major Greene, possessor of an extensive background and valuable experience in things military, made practical application of his knowledge and experience by which his squadron derived innumerable benefits. While his administrative duties absorbed a major portion of his time, nevertheless, he was responsible on numerous occasions for directing other squadron functions. In one major movement, Major Greene commanded a convoy of 136 vehicles on a treacherous 1,200-mile journey from Benghazi to Tunisia. Over shell and bomb torn desert roads, through mine-strewn areas, with few water and petrol points, Major Greene, by skillful planning and ample forethought, brought his convoy through on the allotted schedule of eight days without loss of one vehicle. Although continually handicapped by lack of materials and adequate facilities, Major Greene with his indefatigable spirit has molded his organization into a model squadron. These factors have played a prominent part in establishing the high state of morale and efficiency existing within his squadron. His efforts have been a contributing factor to the outstanding success achieved by his unit in its operations against the enemy and reflect inestimable credit upon himself and the Armed Forces of the United States of America.

In addition, Jim earned the World War II Victory Medal, The American Campaign Medal, the National Defense Service Medal, the Air Force Longevity Service Award and the Armed Forces Reserve Medal with one bronze hourglass device. One bronze hourglass stands for ten years of service. While he didn't have a military career, he served with distinction when the need arose.

Although the war wasn't fought in the United States, Jim was ever mindful of the loss to so many families. He was constantly reminded when he thought of his best friend, Sam, his fellow VMI graduates, and all the comrades he met along his journey. He was never boastful of the 376th accomplishments, realizing how devasting the war was for so many people.

After Japan's surrender, the exuberance in the country was palatable as American society became more affluent. Many returning soldiers took advantage of the G.I. Bill of Rights passed in 1944, providing the means for veterans to attend college to learn new skills, and to purchase homes and farms. Families were formed and careers were established. For those who returned in reasonable health or recovered from their injuries, the positive impact was incalculable.

Many Americans were excluded from this prosperity. Blacks, Hispanics, and women did not have access to the benefits many white men received. As a consequence, they became more determined in trying to seek equality and civil rights leading to the Civil Rights Movement.

Although most Americans felt optimistic, new challenges and perceived threats emerged. By 1948, tensions between the United States and its allies and the Soviet Union and its allies arose. For the next 20 years, the Cold War caused many tensions between the two superpowers in the international sphere.

After settling in Chevy Chase, Jim reacquainted with his extended family and friends. Many afternoons he walked to his cousin's house. The Marshalls and Jim enjoyed discussing the issues of the day. They kept abreast of their cousin, Bishop Albert Rhett Stuart, in Georgia and his work for civil rights. They were always concerned about the future of the country. The older Beale generation resurrected their family gatherings with those still in the area, particularly the Marshalls and Leahys.

Jim reconnected with the VMI community, attending many football and basketball games. He participated in alumni activities in the Washington, D.C. area and helped recruit students. Jim gave moral support to his son, Jimmy, and the younger generation of 3,800 VMI soldiers who served in Vietnam.

Jim set an example of service to others and a focus on a higher purpose for his children.

His oldest son, Jimmy, graduated from the Naval Academy and embarked on a career in the Navy. He married and had two children. His daughter, Margaret Ann, also served in the United States Navy.

Jim's younger son Bill, my father, graduated from VMI and joined Dupont after graduation. He married and had six children and spent his life helping others along life's path.

Jim's daughter, Ann, graduated from Longwood College (now University) as her mother did, and taught U.S. government in North Carolina schools for many years. She had two children, and her daughter taught for 30 years.

Jim welcomed eight of his grandchildren into the world before his death of another heart attack on Oct. 20, 1969. He was buried at Arlington National Cemetery with full military honors among a large crowd of extended family and friends. His wife, Ann, who always supported his decisions, was laid to rest with him on March 17, 1975.